Reaching Out in a Networked World

Reaching Out in a Networked World

*Expressing Your Congregation's
Heart and Soul*

Lynne M. Baab

THE
ALBAN
INSTITUTE

Herndon, Virginia
www.alban.org

The Alban Institute
2121 Cooperative Way, Suite 100
Herndon, VA 20171

Scripture quotations, unless otherwise noted, are from the New Revised Standard Version of the Bible, © 1989, Division of Christian Education of the National Council of Churches of Christ in the United States of America, and are used by permission.

In all stories of individuals, the names and identifying details have been changed or the stories are used with permission.

Cover by Spark Design, LLC.

Library of Congress Cataloging-in-Publication Data

Baab, Lynne M.
  Reaching out in a networked world : expressing your congregation's heart and soul / Lynne M. Baab.
      p. cm.
  Includes bibliographical references.
  ISBN 978-1-56699-368-5
  1. Communication—Religious aspects—Christianity. 2. Information technology—Religious aspects—Christianity. I. Title.

  BV4319.B15 2008
  254'.3—dc22
                              2008023661

        12   11   10   09   08   VP   1   2   3   4   5

Contents

Foreword

WHILE TEACHING AT A CONFERENCE IN NORTH
Carolina, I gathered with church leaders from all over the country
to talk about the future of ministry. In this beautiful setting, with
the clear blue sky above us, and green mountains rolling around
us, it was easy to let our minds wander as we imagined what the
church could be.

Whenever we began to imagine the future of our spiritual communities, the role of communication crept into our conversations.
Shifts are rapidly occurring in technology, so we have many new
ways and opportunities to reach out to our neighbors and tell the
story of our church.

The first time the subject arose was during a conference break.
I relaxed on a couch, eager to catch up with a friend. As I spoke,
this gifted pastor could not understand why I spend a substantial
amount of time writing on a blog each morning. Although we were
both leading a conference on the future of the church, our ideas
on what role technology would play in our upcoming ecclesial
days contrasted greatly. Blogs did not make any sense to my colleague who complained, "They're just full of all kinds of personal
information that I really don't care about. I try to read them, but I
can't find any that are worth my time. I don't know why anyone
visits them."

I tried to explain my own fascination with new media, how
I love to get instant feedback from my writing, and how those
conversations shape my thinking. Reading blogs keeps me

informed about what professional resources are available and what kind of books seminarians read. They even provide a bit of community and support. At this point, I really cannot imagine my professional life without them.

I did not get far in my explanation though, because then the conversation turned to social networking and it stalled even more. I explained that Facebook made it a lot easier for friends to find and contact each other. To which, my friend became utterly perplexed and replied, "It's like having another form of e-mail. I don't want any more e-mail. I don't want anyone else contacting me. I can't keep up with what I have!"

I understand his frustrations. There are many church leaders who already feel too tied to their computer keyboards, and they do not want to spend any more hours in front of their flat, lifeless screens than they have to. They feel like their time scrolling through sites on their computer robs them from real, effective ministry.

Of course, he was not the only conversation partner in all of this. I also met with Bruce Reyes-Chow, the moderator of the Presbyterian Church (USA) and a new church development pastor who is actively engaged with blogs and is caught up in all sorts of social networks. We participated in a podcast, hosted by Shawn Coons and Zach Sasser, talking about young pastors and the Internet. We all agreed that the shifts happening in our culture, especially in the way that we communicate, will have a great effect on our congregations.

Going from one conversation to the next reminded me that I have friends in two camps. One group is fully immersed in the world of technology, as I am. We eat, live, and breathe over some sort of keyboard. The computer is not tied to a desk, and the Internet is not a place that they visit for one hour every day. Rather, a shift happened somewhere in the last decade, and the computer has become an integral part of the whole context of our lives. We can fold up our computers and keep them in our bags. We can even put the Internet in our pockets and practically carry around encyclopedias and full music libraries with us wherever we go.

We have a generally optimistic attitude about technology and all of the gifts that it can bring, and we may even have a tendency to see technology in a utopian sense. Technology is revolutionary. It can flatten structures and dismantle hierarchies. It allows conversation to flow across the globe, so that the brightest minds are no longer hindered by location; rather, they can share information and ideas freely. Ideas and intellectual movements can fly in an instant over continents. With new technologies, we can see how organizing is possible, without the constraints of an organization. Too often we quickly cast aside those who are not so savvy with a website as people who "just don't get it."

The second group is made up of people those who do not understand what is happening, or they feel highly skeptical of the developments. They might see the necessity of a church having a website, but cannot imagine why anyone would want to generate content on a regular basis for it. Social networking irritates them, and participating in blogs just looks like an endless waste of time.

Both types of people were gathered, talking about what church could be. Then there was another voice that I heard at that conference. My friend, Beth Sentell, was there. As a wise pastor and parent, I remember that she gave me some pertinent advice, although it was about an entirely different matter. Beth talked about raising teenagers and said it was always a good idea to drive them places as much as possible.

"There's just something about being in that car," Beth explained. "It's the perfect setting. You're trapped, without much eye contact, and that makes teenagers feel comfortable about telling you stuff. And you just always have to be ready to communicate, when and how they want to."

Although it was mothering advice and not pastoring advice, it rang true as I thought more about the future of our churches. As congregational leaders, we can be prepared to listen and speak when and how people are willing to communicate. In a new generation, that means we can learn to use websites, social networking, e-mails, and desktop publishing to tell the story of our worshiping community most effectively.

To that end, Lynne Baab has written a wonderful and balanced book, full of practical insight. Throughout the pages, she fearlessly explains the direction that we will be going and she gives us the tools to get there. Using *Reaching Out in a Networked World* as a guide, we can learn how to tell the story of who our churches are, but even more than that, we can imagine what our spiritual communities might become, and we can begin to communicate that message in a networked world, in ways that a new generation is ready to hear.

Carol Howard Merritt
Washington, D.C.

Acknowledgments

I AM GRATEFUL TO THE FOLLOWING PEOPLE who talked with me about the issues in this book and gave me many interesting ideas to think about. Fred Westbrook described the audio and video aspects of his work at Duke Chapel and also gave me very helpful feedback on the relevance for congregations of my dissertation research. Deth Im told me about the ways Jacob's Well, Kansas City, Missouri, uses its website to build and nurture connections. John Riemenschnitter talked with me about his goals for The Highway Community Church's (Mountain View, California) website. Alison Link discussed communication strategies at University Presbyterian Church, Seattle, with me. Janet Cawley took the time to brainstorm with me about issues of congregational identity. Tim Cooper talked with me about mission statements and wise use of PowerPoint during worship. Barry Kelk described the way he uses video clips in worship. My writers group, Women Writing Theology, gave me ideas for the second half of chapter 3, and I am grateful to them.

David Domke deserves special mention. He was my doctoral dissertation advisor at the University of Washington, and he helped me in so many ways as I learned to think analytically about websites. When I wrote my dissertation, I interviewed ten people who produce websites for congregations. Their comments and thoughts were very helpful as I wrote this book, and I am grateful to them for their time and insights.

The fifteen students in my course on communication and ministry at the University of Otago in New Zealand gave me quite a few ideas for this book, and the class discussions helped me refine some of my thoughts. Edwina Herring gave a presentation in class about serving people with disabilities, and she looked over my sidebar about people with disabilities and gave me helpful feedback. Thanks, students.

Another group of people have had a lasting impact on my life in areas related to this book. Warm thanks to Joleen Burgess, who designed my own website and who talked with me many times about website issues. I am grateful for the model of Corey Schlosser-Hall and his passion for web-based communication in the years he served Seattle Presbytery as Communications Director. Corey also talked with me about communication mistakes congregations make. Bill Dyrness taught me so much about the visual arts in congregations and connected me with many excellent resources. Steve Hayner has modeled joyful and effective ministry in so many ways for me, and he also talked with me about the ways missional church concerns overlap with the communication tools discussed here.

Three people helped shape this book when it was in manuscript form: Beth Gaede, editor extraordinaire; Jeff Brooks, marketer extraordinaire; and Dave Baab, husband extraordinaire. To you three, thanks so very much.

Introduction

MY HUSBAND AND I RECENTLY MOVED TO A new city. Before we moved, we looked at numerous websites related to our new city, trying to get an idea of what our new home would be like. We pored over websites about tourist activities, the arts community, and the churches in town. When we arrived, we had a small idea of the characteristics of our new hometown.

After our arrival, we visited numerous churches over a period of six months. We wanted to make a wise decision about where we would put down roots, and we also hoped to get a sense of what was going on in the city's churches before we settled into one congregation. With each congregation we visited, we were eager to discover the most significant values of the congregation and what activities they considered to be central to who they were. We also wanted to hear about the priorities and personality of the ministers. What were these congregations and ministers really like?

One of the congregations had a very clear website and welcome brochure, explaining that social justice and music are of central importance to them and that they place a high value on traditional church music performed well. The website and brochure dovetailed well with our experience when we visited.

However, with most of the other churches we visited, finding out what we wanted to know was harder than we expected. Some of the congregations didn't have a website or a brochure for visitors. Many of the congregations that did have websites or brochures gave some basic information about activities but failed to present central values of the congregation. As far as we could tell, none of the ministers had blogs where they discussed their philosophy of ministry and what is important to them about congregational life.

In two cases, we found out later in another setting that the congregations actually had strong priorities—and related programs—that we value highly. When we visited, the congregations' commitment to those priorities was completely invisible.

Based on visits to churches in numerous towns and cities, I believe our experience—and our frustration—would be common in many, if not most, settings. My husband and I are committed churchgoers. We were determined to find a congregation and become involved in it. Our difficulty in discerning the heart and soul of these congregations didn't keep us from continuing to visit and ask questions. But we wondered about people whose commitment to church is more tenuous. What might they feel if they visit a congregation they know nothing about, pick up all the printed material available, visit the website, and then find they still don't know that much about the congregation?

This Book's Emphasis

The central point of this book is that the way congregations communicate their values and identity has become a vitally important concern in our time. This has come about for two reasons. The first reason relates to the recent explosion in communication technologies—e-mail, websites, blogs, podcasts, brochures created with desktop publishing software, social networking websites, projection screens in worship, digital cameras, and many more—which offer a host of new ways to present values and identity. No one has much experience with thinking through the ways congregational values and identity are expressed through these new forms of communication, because so many of these new options simply haven't been around long enough to allow for a great deal of reflection. And congregations often are afraid of new technologies, believe they don't have the money or resources to use them, or don't place a priority on them.

Because of the lack of experience with new forms of communication, many congregations that have websites and brochures don't know how to present a coherent picture of who they are and what they care about. The website, newsletter, and worship bulletin often portray different pictures of the central aspects of the congregation's character, and those pictures may conflict with the message that is communicated by the worship services and ministries of the congregation. Congregations are composed of diverse people with a variety of priorities, and this diversity needs to be expressed. However, each congregation should have a central focus, which is often lacking in the smorgasbord of communication options now available.

A second reason why congregational values and identity are significant in our time comes from societal shifts. Communities of faith are no longer central to the communal life of towns, cities, or rural areas. People no longer feel loyal to the religious institutions of their childhood. In order to provide a coherent and welcoming invitation to the wider community, congregations must be clear about what they value and how they act on those values. And in order to help congregation members grow in their participation in the life of faith, the congregation's leaders need to be persistent in using every possible means of communication about the things that really matter to the congregation.

This book will explore the ways identity and values are expressed in a variety of ways through diverse means of communication. In this introduction, I will address some essential definitions about identity and values and provide some historical background about people of faith and the ways they communicate. The definitions and history will help lay the groundwork for the central issue of this book, the urgency of considering and evaluating the way new technologies can help congregations convey their identity and values to people within and outside the congregation.

What Are Values? What Is Identity?

A congregation's values are simply what it considers to be important—the priorities, principles, and standards around which it centers its life. What spiritual practices are valued in this community? What aspects of a life of faith has this community decided to be intentional about? What are the sources of vitality in this congregation? Congregational values come from a congregation's faith tradition and also from a variety of sources both past and present. A congregation's values are reflected in its plans, priorities, and budget—what it sets out to do in response to its values.

A congregation's values reflect its identity, the aspects of a congregation's character that are central, enduring, and distinctive. A congregation's identity, most simply, is what makes it unique.[1]

Values and identity could be described metaphorically as a congregation's DNA, its heart and soul, or its story. These central characteristics of a congregation are manifested in congregational life in countless ways, intentional and unintentional. They are communicated through words but also through images and actions. In addition, congregational life is full of symbols, ranging from a welcoming new lobby to the elements used in communion services, and these symbols contribute to the communication of the congregation's heart and soul.

Throughout this book I will talk about values and identity, sometimes stressing one, sometimes the other. I see values and identity as intricately related, but not the same thing. The concept of values focuses on what the congregation emphasizes and cares about, while the concept of identity centers on who the congregation is, the aspects of the congregation's character that are central, enduring, and distinctive. Values and identity influence and inform each other, both are expressed in multiple ways in congregations, and both are essential to consider in our time.

Does it really matter if a congregation ignores the possibilities for telling its story using new communication technologies? Isn't it more important simply to get on with the task of being a community of faith? A brief look at the history of engagement with communication issues by people of faith will help give perspective on these new forms of communication.

A Brief History

Throughout history, Jews and Christians have used a variety of means to convey the central aspects of their faith. An overview of some of the ways our faith traditions have utilized various forms of communication will set the groundwork for further exploration.

Judaism is based in the history of a specific people and nation. Therefore, the recording and dissemination of that history has always been significant. The Hebrew Bible was translated into Greek before the birth of Jesus so that Jews who traveled the Roman Empire and spoke Greek could have access to the history of their people and the foundation of their faith tradition in their own language. The Talmud, Mishnah, and Gemara were widely copied and circulated beginning in the second century.

Christians have also been known for using the latest communication technologies to spread the gospel and to nurture faith. In the fourth century, Augustine applied principles of classical rhetoric, a secular discipline, to the analysis of biblical texts and preaching, and for the next thousand years such analysis was common throughout Europe. In the fifteenth century, the Bible was one of the earliest books to be printed on the newly invented printing press, and in the early years of printing, Christians and Jews printed simple booklets and sermons. As printing became more common and sophisticated, a range of Christian and Jewish material was printed, including magazines, newspapers, and books on a variety of topics related to issues of faith. When radio and television were introduced, Jews and Christians immediately saw the opportunity to make use of these technologies.

The rapid adoption of Internet-based communication and digital technologies by some communities of faith stands in a long tradition of enthusiastically embracing new means of communication to spread the gospel and nurture faith communities. At the same time, the skepticism about these technologies, and the concern about possible dangers and abuses, stands in an equally long tradition. A pertinent illustration of these concerns and skepticism dates from the invention of the telephone. At that time, numerous voices in the press, in academic communities, and in various faith traditions expressed concern that the telephone would damage human communication because nonverbal cues are not accessible by telephone. There was a danger, some people said, of losing a commitment to human community. Good relationships might be damaged because of impersonal voices over a phone line.

Anyone who has lived hundreds or thousands of miles away from loved ones can testify to the power of telephones to nurture relationships, not damage them. But anyone who has experienced repeated phone calls interrupting dinner discussion can also attest to the necessity of discussing guidelines for telephone use. The newest communication technologies present the same kinds of opportunities for nurturing community as well as dangers from unwise use.

Why Do Identity and Values Matter?

Diana Butler Bass, a scholar who specializes in the study of American religion and culture, has identified three characteristics of healthy congregations: intentionality, practice, and vitality.[2] Healthy congregations are *intentional* about the ways they nurture spiritual life. They encourage basic spiritual *practices*—prayer, Scripture reading, and service—in a variety of ways for individuals and for communities of people. They also encourage a variety of spiritual *practices* that grow out of prayer and Scripture study, such as hospitality, generosity, Sabbath keeping, storytelling, and discernment. Such intentionality and practice result in *vitality* in congregational life.

Another way to describe healthy Christian congregations is that they are *missional*. Their leaders and members understand that the church is not a building, a program, or a worship service; instead, they know their congregation exists to participate in God's mission in the world. They believe their call is to see what God is doing in the world, to allow their hearts to be broken by the things that break God's heart, and to point out and join God's work.[3]

A congregation's communication plays a significant role in reflecting and nurturing intentionality, practice, vitality, and a missional perspective. I am particularly interested in the role played by new communication tools such as websites, blogs, e-mail, and social networking websites in communicating identity and values. I will also discuss the changes in communication in recent decades that are exercising a significant impact on congregations, such as the rise of visual communication and the significance of telling stories rather than recounting principles. These discussions will provide a model for the way new and emerging communication technologies—ones that no one has even dreamed of yet—can be evaluated for their potential to communicate values and identity. I will begin in the next chapter by describing my own journey related to these issues.

Questions for Reflection, Journaling, and Discussion

1. Make a list of five or ten values that you believe are most significant in your congregation. Where do you see those values communicated clearly? Which values get the least attention? Which ones get the most attention?

2. What aspects of your congregation's life do you consider to be central, enduring, and distinctive? In what ways and places are those aspects of congregational life communicated the most clearly?

3. Spend some time reflecting on the three words used by Diana Butler Bass to describe healthy congregations: intentionality, practice, and vitality. What do they mean to you? What do they look like in your congregation? In what ways are they missing in your congregation? In what ways do they connect to your congregation's values and identity?

1 | Paradigm Shifts in Communication

A Personal Journey

THE EXPLORATION OF CONGREGATIONAL identity and congregational communication in this book comes largely out of four experiences in my life during the past eighteen years. Because those experiences dovetail with some of the major shifts in communication that have occurred over recent decades, I want to recount my experiences here and reflect on their significance.

I attended seminary in the 1980s when my children were young, taking ten years to finish a three-year degree. When I graduated in 1990, I knew I still wasn't ready to be ordained as a pastor, so I worked for six years for my local presbytery and synod, both of them headquartered in my home city, Seattle. I created publications—doing the writing, editing, and layout of a bimonthly newspaper, a quarterly newsletter, numerous brochures and booklets, and even placemats with games for children and the young at heart.

First Experience: Fonts, Layout, and Graphics

When I took the writing-editing-formatting jobs with the presbytery and synod, I had virtually no experience with creating printed publications. I had been an enthusiastic reader of books, newspapers, and magazines my whole life, so I had my opinions about what I liked to read and what text should look like. I had written a handful of articles for magazines, so I had some experience with writing for publication. I had been an elder in a Presbyterian congregation and I had a seminary degree, so I knew something about church leadership.

I dived into the task of writing articles about what congregations in my region were doing. In those six years of writing articles, I learned about amazing and wonderful ministries in congregations as well as complex and heartbreaking issues that congregational leaders face. I also gained expertise in making writing vivid. I learned about useful writing skills like the power of active verbs and the importance of varying sentence length. My growing understanding of congregational life and my growing abilities to write clearly built on the skills I had when I took those jobs.

New learning came from developing skills in desktop publishing. I attended workshops on creating newsletters and brochures, and I began to observe printed publications with new eyes. I noticed that the choice of fonts communicates something visually that can complement or undercut the words chosen. I learned that layout does the same thing. I had exhilarating moments in those six years when I created an inviting and readable layout that I felt perfectly complemented the content of an article or announcement.

I was slower to gain competence with photos and graphics. The Presbyterian Church (U.S.A.) sent us lots of graphics and photos to use in our publications, and I felt overwhelmed by most of them. However, one year in the fall, they sent a graphic of a nativity scene in which Mary, Joseph, and Jesus were clearly Native American. I used it in the synod newspaper, and I pondered it long afterward. It made me think about the Native American perspective and social justice in a new light. In a small way, I began to see the significance of visual resources.

When I left the synod and presbytery jobs, I considered myself to be somewhat competent in desktop publishing. I knew how to create readable publications in which the verbal text was clear and well complemented by the layout and font choices. I could see that photos and graphics were significant, but I often felt intimidated about the best way to use them. I lacked knowledge about how to "read" them and how they interacted with verbal text.

Second Experience: Wrestling with Congregational Identity

In 1997 I was ordained to serve as an associate pastor at a lively urban Presbyterian church in Seattle, where I served for seven years. My job description covered several areas of congregational life, including overseeing all of the congregation's communication. I began by revamping the format of the congregation's monthly newsletter. Then I turned my attention to the various brochures and other printed material.

The congregation had a welcome brochure that gave basic information about the congregation's ministries, priorities, and membership. Copies of the welcome brochure sat on a table in the lobby of the fellowship hall.

As I prepared to create a new design for that brochure, the senior pastor suggested that I also make welcome cards that would fit in the pew racks. He and I decided the welcome brochure and the welcome cards should have a similar look. I picked half a dozen fonts that I thought communicated something of the congregation's blend of informality and tradition, and the senior pastor picked the one he liked best. I used that font for headers for both the brochure and the card.

What should go on the card? We decided on a statement of welcome and a list of a few of the congregation's ministries on the front, with the names, area of responsibility, and contact information of the pastoral staff listed on the back. We decided to use a header on the front saying, "What's going on here?" We hoped those words communicated something of the congregation's willingness to answer questions, and when I formatted the cards I curved the words so that they looked playful.

As I considered how to create the brochure and card, I spent a lot of time pondering who we were as a congregation and how the various components of paper-based communication could reflect that identity. I liked the font we had chosen for the headers because I thought it reflected who the congregation was, and making the text curved rather than straight seemed to convey something significant about the congregation's flexibility and creativity. A graphic artist in the congregation had designed a terrific logo for the congregation a year or two before, and so I put the logo on the card and the brochure. We had chosen appropriate text for both the brochure and the card; it was brief, succinct, and descriptive of the congregation's various activities and ministries.

But something was still lacking. I didn't want to use photos, because the card and brochure would be photocopied, and photos often don't photocopy well. And I was still intimidated by photos; I didn't think I knew how to use them well. I didn't want to use clip art, because it is so often kitschy, and while this was an informal congregation, it was also highly educated. Cutesy graphics didn't seem to fit with the nature of who we were.

I thought a lot about that pew card. I could picture a newcomer or visitor pulling it out of the pew rack while waiting for the worship service to start. As they scanned it briefly, what would their eye land on? I envisioned someone who had been attending the church for a year or two reading the card while the offering was being collected. What would strike them about the card and about the congregation? I could imagine long-time members looking at the card. What faith practices might be encouraged?

I thought about some of the central activities of the congregation, and I asked an artist in the congregation if she would create some simple line drawings for the card and brochure: a cup of coffee, a globe, some bars of music, and a pot of soup with a ladle beside it. Her style is casual and contemporary, and the graphics proved to be exactly what was lacking. I used the cup of coffee and the bars of music on the welcome card. For the welcome brochure, I placed the cup of coffee beside some text about small groups, the bars of music close to text about the worship service, the globe next to text about the missions and outreach programs, and the pot of soup and ladle near information about fellowship events.

From my point of view, the welcome card and brochure communicated a lot about this particular congregation, and communicated it well. Both values and activities were discussed verbally and portrayed visually. The verbal text, graphics, fonts, and layout contributed to communicating the essence of who this congregation was. Visitors, new attenders, and even people who had been there a while would be able to learn something about the congregation.

In my seven years as an associate pastor, I spent a fair amount of time wrestling with how best to communicate the identity of this congregation in written publications. I grew more competent using graphics and photos, but my central love was words and how they were placed on pages. During my years at the church, a group of volunteers created a website, and I talked with them occasionally regarding the website, but that was another area where I was slow to get engaged.

In those years I believed that the identity of a congregation could be discovered, that the task of the brochure maker or bulletin designer was to try to discern who the congregation is and reflect that reality in publications. I didn't understand that identity is at least in part constructed by the people producing the publications—me! I had a vague sense that the brochures and other publications I was creating would play a part in shaping the way people thought about the congregation, but I didn't realize how significant that aspect of communication is.

Third Experience:
Visiting Lots of Congregations

When I left my position as associate pastor in 2004, I spent more than a year visiting congregations all around Seattle. In fifteen months I visited more than two dozen congregations, most of them

VISUAL LITERACY

"The primary literacy of the 21st century will be visual: pictures, graphic, images of every kind" (p. 1). So argues Lynell Burmark in her book *Visual Literacy: Learn to See, See to Learn*. She is an educational consultant who believes that students need to be taught visual literacy as a part of learning to communicate in the twenty-first century, and she argues that teachers need to understand visual literacy in order to teach more effectively.

Burmark notes that our need to learn visual literacy arises because images were relatively rare until recently. The rise of electricity made movies, television, and the digital era possible.

Visual literacy has two major components: learning to "read" or interpret visual images and learning to use visual images to communicate. Burmark amplifies these two components into four characteristics of a visually literate person, who should be able to:

- "Interpret, understand, and appreciate the meaning of visual images;
- "Communicate more effectively by applying the basic principles and concepts of visual design;
- "Produce visual messages using computers and other technologies; and
- "Use visual thinking to conceptualize solutions to problems" (p. 3).

These skills, Burmark believes, are increasingly important in most workplaces.

Burmark discusses the ways images are interpreted, the significance of typefaces as unconscious persuaders, the power of color to communicate, the use of charts, and some of the implications of digital technologies. She considers visual literacy to be the "3-D eyeglasses for the mind, the lenses through which we see the meaning—the words and ideas—behind the images" (p. 101). (Alexandria, VA: Association for Supervision and Curriculum Development, 2002) two or three times. About half were Presbyterian, but I also visited numerous other denominations and independent churches.

I had left my associate pastor position to enter full-time doctoral studies in communication at the University of Washington, en route to a teaching position. That first year of doctoral study was amazingly humiliating because I had so much to learn about the field of communication. But every Sunday I was back in a comfortable church milieu, observing hundreds of details about each congregation.

As I sat in one unfamiliar church after another, I tried to notice all the clues that gave me information about the distinctive features of that congregation. One of them had the most amazing stained-glass windows showing heroes of the civil rights movement. I wondered how much those windows reflected the current values of the congregation. Another one had a team of four ministers who shared the preaching equally. I wondered if that kind of equality in teamwork filtered through all the congregation's activities. In one church, the minister thanked the children for being there before she dismissed them to the children's activities. Her brief words of thanks seemed to honor the children in a significant way and communicate something about her values. Did those values extend to the congregation as a whole as they ministered with children?

I looked at the information each church had on its welcome table or in display cases. I examined the cards and envelopes in the pew racks. I carefully read the worship bulletin. I listened to the verbal announcements made from the front of the church and watched the images and words on the projection screen if one was used. After the service, I often visited the congregation's website to see if what the website communicated paralleled or contradicted what I had experienced in worship.

After each visit I noted what I had learned about the congregation and I tried to discern where I had learned it. Often I noticed a conflict between what I perceived about the congregation's values and identity from attending one or two worship services and what I read in brochures or saw on its website. Sometimes the brochure and the website contradicted each other. I began to realize, more than ever before, that everything about a church communicates something, and I saw that conflicting messages about a congregation are confusing to a visitor. I was deeply curious about how congregations could do a better job communicating what they care about and who they view themselves to be.

As the time approached for me to choose a topic for my doctoral dissertation, I decided to focus on congregational websites and look specifically at how congregations express their identity on their websites. Despite my passion for paper publications, I could see clearly that websites would soon eclipse brochures and newsletters, and I wanted to learn more about how they worked and what they could do for congregations.

Fourth Experience: Absorption in Websites

I spent the better part of two years looking at websites created by Protestant Christian churches in the United States. When I set up the research design for my dissertation, I was committed to studying the websites as visual objects, not just collections of words. Some earlier studies of websites examined the words used on the sites. My experience with desktop publishing had taught me that the appearance of words is just as significant as what they say, so I was committed to analyzing the look of the sites as well as the words they used.

Still not feeling confident about my ability to understand the significance of photos and graphics, I read widely about visual culture. I learned that the advertising industry paved the way in using visual images strategically. Writer after writer talked about the worldwide rise in use of visual images in almost every form of communication over the past few decades. We have shifted from being a word-based culture to becoming a visual culture, they said. I learned that the word *text* no longer applies only to words. Photos and graphics are also texts—visual texts—that need to be read and analyzed in a similar way to verbal texts.

FONTS ON WEBSITES SPEAK

I recently looked at the home page of a congregational website. The congregation's name was written in an elegant script font. I don't know the name of that particular font, but I liked it very much. It was elegant in a contemporary way, and in my mind it evoked a twenty-first-century formal wedding with classical music, women in beautiful, trendy dresses, and great food spread out on tables with Japanese flower arrangements and avant-garde ice sculptures. The use of that font for the name of a congregation aroused curiosity in me; I wondered in what ways that congregation might be like a beautiful contemporary wedding. The congregation had a concise mission statement, appropriate and effective for a website. Unfortunately, the person who designed that website had chosen to put the mission statement in Comic Sans right below the congregation's name. Comic Sans is one of the most informal fonts available and looks like the writing used in goofy comic strips. The juxtaposition of the voice of those two fonts—elegant and goofy—gave a strong impression that the congregation didn't have the faintest idea who they were, and so they were trying to cover all bases. A generous observer might argue that the use of two such opposite fonts could represent the diversity present in the congregation, but my first impression was of confusion. As I continued to look at that web page, my sense of confusion didn't go away, and I was simply not able to focus on the lovely and appropriate words of the mission statement. The confusing message communicated by the fonts was louder than the message about the identity of the congregation communicated in words.

I interviewed some of the people who produced the websites I studied. In most cases, one individual produced the website for the congregation. They often got verbal text from the staff or leaders of the congregation, but usually one person made the decisions regarding photos, layout, fonts, and colors. All of those choices communicate significant things, and I found myself wondering how one person could accurately represent a congregation's values and identity. What about other points of view about who the congregation is and what it cares about?

My research called into question my own practice as an associate pastor. I had collaborated with the senior pastor in creating brochures and other publications, but did the two of us make decisions that accurately communicated the values of this congregation? How much did my own taste influence the choice of text, graphics, fonts, and layout? But if collaboration about the appearance of publications is a good idea, how does that work in practice? After all, verbal text produced by groups of people tends to be bland and often convoluted. Wouldn't the same be true of visual texts?

Throughout most of the writing of my dissertation, I still believed that a congregation has an identity that needs to be discovered and communicated through publications and actions. It took me a long time to begin to perceive that identity is also shaped and constructed through the use of communication, action, and symbols.

When a minister talks frequently in sermons about the significant commitment to prayer in this congregation, members begin to see themselves as people who value prayer. The frequent mention of events centered around prayer and the use of banners or projection screen images that represent prayer visually may nudge members towards a view that this congregation is a place where people pray and this congregation is composed of people who enjoy and value prayer. Congregation members will probably find themselves choosing to pray more often. Time and again, what we hear, see, and read influences us as we interpret our experiences and choose ways to respond.

A congregation's identity as the essence of who it is may exist in God's mind, but every member of a congregation will have a different perception of what that essence is. Therefore part of our task as leaders is to be careful about all the ways the identity of the congregation gets constructed through the congregation's communication and actions, and the symbols it uses.

The Shift from Words Alone to Words and Images

I still love words. I know that words will probably remain my first love for a long time. I am not unique as a person in ministry in my love of words. Many people in leadership positions take joy in crafting words into sermons and articles. We will spend significant time striving for a well-chosen word that will capture and express the idea we are mulling over.

The four experiences I have recounted shaped me significantly and have given me pause about spending so much time focused on words. If advertising research is accurate, visual components almost always have a more immediate impact on viewers than verbal components. I now understand that a visitor's initial assessment of a congregation's values may be influenced most by the artwork displayed in the lobby, the graphic on the cover of a bulletin, or the image used on a website. The furniture and layout of the lobby itself may make the strongest impression.

If it is true that many visual components of congregation life have a significant impact, then this has profound implications for congregations. It calls into question the long-standing pattern of ministers and staff members generating verbal text for brochures, websites, and projection screens in worship, while someone else, often not even a member of the congregation, designs the layout and chooses fonts, photos, and graphics. It raises questions about the interpretation of images. One image can have a variety of meanings. If communities of faith move towards increasing use of images, will the result be that meaning becomes diffuse and anything goes? One website designer who I interviewed for my dissertation research talked about the few images she uses on the congregational website she designed and maintained. She said she wanted website viewers to concentrate on the message of the church, which she believed was communicated best through words on the website and through sermon downloads. She thinks images contribute to a "flashy" image, which contradicts the message of the congregation.

That website did a good job communicating the congregation's values verbally. However, it was not very attractive on first glance. I don't know if a potential visitor would spend much time at the site because of its lack of images. I admired that web designer's careful thinking about her strategy, but I wasn't sure if she had made the right choice. Her choice certainly raises questions about how congregational leaders can best respond to the move toward visual communication.

I still affirm the significance of words to describe aspects of congregational life accurately. Words specify actions and responses that are desired by congregational leaders, they anchor photographs and images with an interpretation of their meaning, and they provide precise descriptions of the life of faith. But I now see more clearly that images and photographs, and the overall look of things, need to be considered as seriously as the words that describe them.

Other Shifts

I am still learning new aspects of the change from verbal to verbal and visual communication. For my generation, so strongly word based, the implications of the shift will probably play out in many ways for many years. I emphasized that shift as I described some of the stages of my personal journey, but other shifts were also occurring as I learned about congregational life and good communication.

This is a time of rapid change, which affects communities of faith in a variety of ways. Since 1997, when I began overseeing a congregation's communication efforts, I have written six books on Christian spiritual disciplines and on congregational leadership. The books were based heavily on interviews, and listening to the stories told by people in congregations has made several other shifts clear to me. Studying websites for my doctoral dissertation, along with interviewing some of the people who produce those websites, has confirmed the significance of these additional shifts.

From Principles to Stories

One of the characteristics of communication in a postmodern age is the significance of stories. Just like images, they can be read different ways, giving hearers or readers responsibility to provide their own interpretation. The level of engagement that is required to create one's own interpretation is part of the reasons why stories, like images, have an impact that is often longer lasting than words. We engage with stories, therefore we remember them.

Some of the websites I studied featured stories, sometimes brief and sometimes quite long, of people in the congregations. When I look back on those many months of studying websites, I remember visual images and stories most of all. Lists of principles, common on congregational websites, don't stick in my mind as profoundly.

Congregations can make space for storytelling in worship services, at annual meetings, in printed publications, on websites and blogs, in small groups, and in a number of other settings. Stories can convey the vitality of a journey of faith. Stories teach values in a way that is effective in our time and must play a significant role in communicating the heart and soul of a congregation's life.

From the Individual to Life in Community

As I interviewed people in congregations for articles and books and as I studied congregational communication for my doctorate, I heard a strong longing for life in community. The individualism in Western culture has grown to unhealthy proportions, and people

INTEGRITY IN STORYTELLING

Rose had been struggling for a long time to resolve a conflict with her father, and she decided to talk to her minister about it. A few weeks later, the minister told a story in his sermon about a conflict between a woman and her father. Rose was furious that her confidentiality had been violated. She went to her minister to confront him, and he assured her he was telling someone else's story and that he had asked permission to do so.

Rose will never know if the minister was telling the truth or not, but her anger raises a significant issue in an age where stories of faith journeys are becoming increasingly important. If someone is telling her own story, obviously no permission needs to be asked, unless her story involves personal details about other people. But if another person's story is told, obtaining permission to tell the story is essential. This matters in a sermon that is not recorded in any way, and it matters even more now that sermons are posted on websites in written or oral form and circulated well beyond the original intended audience.

This raises the question about telling a child or teenager's story. At what age can a child or teenager give informed consent? Is it morally acceptable for a parent to give permission to tell a child's story? I believe it is wise to err on the cautious side in order to honor the faith journey of children and teenagers.

Asking permission to tell other people's stories shows respect for the autonomy and integrity of those individuals. When asking people to tell their own personal stories orally or in writing, be sure to ask them if there are other people involved in the story from whom it might be wise to ask permission.

in faith communities seem to be more explicit in their desire to reclaim the communal emphasis of a life of faith that has been significant from the very origins of Jewish and Christian faith traditions. On the websites I studied, the language of welcome, belonging, relationships, connection, and community was common.

Community in congregations is taking new forms. Fellowship groups and small group Bible studies still exist and, in many cases, thrive. In addition, new groups are forming around contemplative prayer, local and international outreach, and care for the poor. Groups focused on a plethora of special interests, such as parenting, adoption, aging, and surviving cancer, are proliferating. A movement among young people, often called the new monasticism, stresses ancient spiritual disciplines such as fasting and service that are exercised in community with the goal of showing God's love in the world. Community is also moving online, with online support groups and social networking websites providing connections that often feel just as significant as face-to-face relationships. In addition, forms of online communication increasingly supplement and nurture face-to-face relationships.

In the light of the loneliness and isolation so frequently described in the media, communities of faith have wonderful opportunities to offer relational connections in a variety of ways, connections that will empower individuals and groups to look beyond themselves and see the places where God is already working in the world. New forms of communication can help facilitate community, and we will explore some of those ways in this book.

From Religious Institution to Community of Faith

For the churches of Western culture, the signs of post-Christendom include fewer people attending church because they feel they should do so. More people attend because they want to be there. This has resulted in a shift away from congregations as societal institutions where people go through the motions of faith. Instead, all across the theological spectrum, I have sensed in interviews a desire on the part of interviewees for communities where real faith is lived out.

Spiritual disciplines are becoming more important again, including the basic spiritual disciplines of prayer, Bible study, and service, as well as Sabbath keeping, fasting, discernment, generosity, and a host of others. Even within the basic practices of prayer and Bible study, many new methods are being discussed and promoted, ranging from praying with icons to *lectio divina*, an ancient practice of meditating on the Bible. A number of these spiritual disciplines can be exercised in the company of others as well as alone. All of these spiritual disciplines—solitary and communal—are bringing vitality to congregations in the post-Christendom age.

Because spiritual disciplines connect us with God's heart and priorities, they have an impact on relationships and the call to serve with love in the world. Healthy communities of faith look beyond themselves to engage with the needs of the wider world because of God's care for all people.

As congregations consider who they are and who they want to be in this post-Christendom era, a commitment to nurturing real faith in real community is essential. This commitment must be communicated as a central component of the values and identity of the congregation, and the specifics of what faith and community look like in each congregation must be highlighted.

From Emphasis on Appearances to Desire for Authenticity

The word *authenticity* appeared frequently on the websites I studied, particularly in the churches with a large number of younger people, indicating a shift away from the need to keep up appearances. What conveys authenticity? Personal stories play a significant role, along with the affirmation that questions are welcome, that doubt can be a teacher in the life of faith, and that mistakes help people grow.

Authenticity was defined vividly on one website I studied: "We as a church are called to be real. We strive to be WYSIWYG

(What You See Is What You Get)."[1] Another website furthered that definition: "We are also authentic. We believe that God is honored and lives are transformed when people are honest, genuine, and real, exposing their brokenness to God and to others. We try not to wear masks."[2]

For congregations that attract younger people, authenticity is linked to community. Numerous websites I studied expressed the view that without authenticity, community is meaningless. If communities of faith are going to become communities that welcome younger people, then a careful consideration of how to become more committed to authenticity will be essential, and a strategic communication of that commitment will also be significant.

From an Emphasis on Unity to Unity and Diversity

The embrace of cultural diversity in recent decades has brought color and vibrancy to Christians in Western cultures as we have adopted worship styles and many forms of artistic expression from around the world. The flowering of interest in spiritual gifts and personality type in recent decades has given vocabulary to describe human differences in positive and constructive ways. These changes have brought profound changes to congregations, changes that mirror the priorities of the New Testament.

First Corinthians 12:4-7 talks about the tension that all churches now need to embrace: they worship one God and affirm one faith, but they celebrate members' and participants' numerous gifts and diverse ways of serving, and they embrace the variety of activities that can come from one faith and one God. In a culture that emphasizes diversity without unity, faith communities can bring the gift of affirming that God provides a place of peaceful and loving unity in the midst of glorious and vibrant diversity.

This has profound implications for all congregational communications. Newsletters, websites, brochures, and other forms of communication need to present a coherent picture of the faith priorities that draw the congregation together in unity, while also reflecting the diversity of congregational life.

When I visited a couple dozen congregations in Seattle a few years ago, I found that some congregations were confusing. The worship service and the publications presented different and contradictory views of what the congregation's priorities were. Unity was missing, and it wasn't clear to me that the diversity I saw in the publications actually reflected the diversity in the congregation.

Unity is essential but must not be overemphasized; diverse activities and ways of serving are also a significant aspect of congregational life. Photos often do a good job of illustrating various components of congregational life without needing to use a lot of words. Holding unity and diversity in tension, rather than emphasizing just one of them, is another shift that needs to be front and center as congregations think about presenting their identity.

The Significance of These Shifts

These shifts are essential to keep in mind as congregational leaders consider how intentionality, practice, and vitality can be nurtured through the ways they are communicated. No congregation can do everything. And effective communication is specific and concrete. Therefore congregations need to figure out what they value in each of these areas so that the uniqueness of their approach can be communicated.

What small groups and fellowship groups does the congregation offer? What groups focused on specific needs are available? What other opportunities for community exist? What specific forms of outreach to the community and world does this congregation engage in, and in what ways does that engagement foster congregational community and intentional spiritual growth? What specific spiritual disciplines are most commonly practiced and encouraged in the congregation? In what settings in this community of faith are real life stories told? What does authenticity look like in this community of faith? In what ways is the unity of the congregation held in tension with its diversity?

Being intentional in conveying these and other values helps people outside the congregation understand the uniqueness of this community, the practices that have shaped this community and continue to shape it. Intentional communication of the congregation's values and identity helps people within the congregation grab hold of the concrete faith values that lead to spiritual vitality.

This intentional communication has to take into account many new practicalities: the readability of verbal text, the choice of photos and graphics, and the opportunities provided by websites, blogs, and online connection. These have come into view because of new communication technologies, and they stand alongside the way congregations have always communicated their values and identity through sermons, worship services, newsletter articles, ministries, and physical space in the building.

Choosing to be intentional about communication also requires that congregational leaders and members examine the underlying presuppositions that influence their thoughts and actions. In the next chapter, I will discuss a series of myths that can impede vital and effective communication in congregations.

Questions for Reflection, Journaling, and Discussion

1. In what ways have you seen an increase in visual communication and a decrease in emphasis on words, both in our culture and in congregations? What have you experienced as the benefits and costs of this change?
2. This chapter describes numerous shifts that have occurred in recent decades in congregations. Which of the changes have you observed and where have you observed them? Do you disagree that some of them have occurred? If so, why? What do you think are the benefits of these changes for your congregation? The dangers? The implications? In what ways could your community of faith do a better job of responding to these shifts?

3. Look back at your own personal journey. What are some
    of the factors that have shaped your views on congre-
    gational communication the most profoundly? In what
    ways have those changes affected your participation in
    your community of faith?

2 | Myths about Identity, Values, and Communication

EVERYTHING ABOUT A CONGREGATION SPEAKS of its values. Imagine walking into a church you know nothing about. If you see children's art posted on bulletin boards, hear the happy voices of kids singing and playing, and see announcements for youth choirs, youth trips, and children's performances, you will know something about that church. It supports its families.

In the same way, displays about mission trips or international development programs communicate engagement with the wider world. Discussion in sermons about spiritual disciplines speaks of a commitment to a life of faith. In recent years, many congregations have added a large lobby or narthex, because at least in part they know that a welcoming place conveys the congregation's desire to welcome people.

A congregation's publications speak of its values as well. Bulletins, brochures, websites, and outdoor signs are intended as communication tools, and they do indeed convey much about the congregation. They reveal aspects of the congregation's life through titles of sermons and classes, descriptions of upcoming events, photos of congregational activities, and even the general feel and layout. Congregations often create mission and vision statements to express their priorities.

For generations, congregational leaders have known that decisions about programs, building, worship style, outreach, and publications have significance. They have known, on a conscious or unconscious level, that those decisions communicate important

things about a congregation to the people within the congregation and to the wider community. They have made conscious and
careful choices in many areas in order to express the central values
that come from their faith.

Changes in communication technology make these decisions
much more complex today. Past generations had to rely on graphic
designers because they weren't able to create their own advertisements for the yellow pages or the local newspaper or make their
own brochures. Now desktop publishing software makes all sorts
of in-house publications possible. The powerful desktop publishing tools available are often used by people with no training in
design, layout, and editing, and the congregational leaders who
oversee the publications have usually spent little time thinking
about the theological and practical implications of the use of such
tools.

Many additional communication technologies are also new.
Past generations didn't have the option of using websites or blogs
or podcasted sermons or video projection during worship. They
couldn't take digital photos of congregational activities and print
the photos—or e-mail them, post them on a website, or send them
on a cell phone—just seconds later. Most of these options didn't
exist twenty years ago, and some of them didn't exist five or ten
years ago. People of faith have only begun to consider the theological implications and wise use of these options.

Explosion is the best word to describe what has happened in
the field of communication in recent years. As one new technology
after another has appeared on the scene, some communities of
faith have enthusiastically embraced the possibilities. Others are
wary or even bewildered by the options. In every case, no matter
how many new technologies have been adopted, congregational
leaders have no long-term experience with assessing the effectiveness of their use.

Websites, digital photos, blogs, sermon downloads, social
networking websites, and other new communication options offer
a congregation a wonderful opportunity to consider the implications of all the ways it can express who it is and what it values.

OPTIONS FOR EXPLORING IDENTITY

Numerous books offer fascinating and helpful methods for exploring congregational identity:

Who Is Our Church? Imagining Congregational Identity by Janet R. Cawley (The Alban Institute, 2006) describes a process of comparing a congregation to a person with gender, age, and other specific characteristics. Cawley's method has the advantage of being playful, creative, and nonthreatening, and it enables congregation members to think outside the box and come up with insights that are relatively free from "shoulds" and "oughts."

Appreciative inquiry is a method of inquiring into what people most appreciate and value about an organization. *The Power of Appreciative Inquiry: A Practical Guide to Positive Change* by Diana Whitney and Amanda Trosten-Bloom (Berrett-Koehler Communications, 2003) is a good introduction to this method. Mark Lau Branson's book, *Memories, Hopes, and Conversations: Appreciative Inquiry and Congregational Change* (The Alban Institute, 2004), offers an account of how one Presbyterian church used appreciative inquiry to bring about positive change.

Systems theory has been long used to describe congregations as complex systems. *Treasures in Clay Jars: New Ways to Understand Your Church* by George B. Thompson Jr. (Pilgrim Press, 2003) draws on insights from psychology, sociology, and anthropology to help congregational leaders explore their congregation's identity.

Other books that are helpful in exploring congregational identity include *The Hidden Lives of Congregations: Understanding Church Dynamics* by Israel Galindo (The Alban Institute, 2004) and *Congregation and Community*, edited by Nancy Tatom Ammerman (Rutgers University Press, 2001), which has a terrific list of questions in an appendix to use in discussions about how a congregation works.

Both values and identity take on new significance due to changes in communication options.

Some Myths

Congregational leaders have been making decisions—both consciously and unconsciously—for decades about identity and values and how they are communicated. The nine myths below lay out some of the underlying issues that may influence these conscious and unconscious choices.

Myth 1

We've got a mission statement, so we've figured out who we are.
Mission (or vision) statements can be helpful to congregations in expressing who they are and what they care about. Leaders and members are tempted to believe that once a mission statement is in place, the congregation can get on with doing ministry. A mission statement, however, is simply one small way among many that a congregation can communicate its heart and soul. In fact, everything about a congregation communicates. Bulletins, newsletters, and websites may use a mission statement, but the photos, layout, and additional text also contribute to the reader's perception of who this congregation is. The actions of a congregation—its worship style, preaching, ministries, and mission activities—speak of its DNA, its story. All of the congregation's communication needs to be evaluated from time to time to see if all of it reflects the values and identity of the congregation.

Myth 2

Our identity is rooted in our faith.
Leaders and members are tempted to believe that they don't need to spend time considering the specific identity of their congregation, because their faith values provide the DNA for their congregation. And it is absolutely true that in communities of faith,

identity comes primarily from the congregation's faith tradition. Faith communities are not businesses or other organizations that need to create an identity from scratch. However, in the same way that individuals within any faith tradition bring specific gifts in service, so faith communities have particular values and emphases. This one might have a strong commitment to justice, another one to outreach within the local community, another one to ministry with seniors or teenagers or adoptive families. Sometimes it appears that megachurches can do it all, and so congregational leaders might think their congregation should do everything too. But even megachurches have particular emphases and priorities.

Myth 3

If we focus too much on figuring out our own identity, we may become self-absorbed.
This is another statement with some truth to it, but not the whole truth. Congregational identity is only part of what congregational leaders should be attending to. While focusing on it all the time would definitely cause an imbalance, my observation is that many congregations are out of balance now in that they focus too little on the way their actions, publications, and use of symbols communicate their priorities and the distinctiveness of who they are. "Who are we and what are we about?" is a key question that needs to be front and center for all congregations.

Myth 4

We don't need to think any further about the implications of new communication technology because we already use it well.
A number of congregations have mastered necessary skills related to new forms of communication in admirable ways. Many congregations offer podcasted and streaming video sermons on websites, they have wonderful teams of people who run the data projectors on Sunday morning, and they embrace new communication technologies as they emerge. But that doesn't mean they are communicating wisely. In some congregations, the message

communicated about values differs from one mode of communication to the next because the various forms of communication haven't been evaluated well. In other congregations, the message is so unified that the congregation's diversity is not represented well. Focusing on the deeper questions, the issues that lie behind the use of new technologies, is important. Congregational leaders need to consider the ways everything the congregation does—communication technologies as well as things like programming and the use of physical space in the building—speak about the congregation's priorities.

Myth 5

We're a traditional congregation, and we have chosen not to use most of the new communication technologies. We've figured out our identity; it's the same as it's always been, so why complicate things?

All congregations need to rethink and explore who they are and what they value from time to time. Even if all the people attending a congregation stayed the same over a decade, each of those people would have undergone personal changes in that time, and those personal changes would change the priorities and emphases of that community of faith. And, of course, no congregation keeps the same members over a decade or more. The flow of people in and out of a congregation, and in and out of leadership roles, shapes the values of each congregation. And while I do think new communication technologies offer some wonderful opportunities for congregations, I would never argue that congregations need to use all of them. I am arguing that everything congregations say and do contributes to their identity. Therefore paying some attention to the issue is wise, no matter what forms of communication are used.

Myth 6

We avoid the new technologies because we're leery of the consumer culture, and we don't want our congregation and even our faith to turn into yet one more consumer item.

I am concerned that communities of faith have become consumer items and that people looking for a congregation are engaged in a form of shopping. However, I see congregational identity as an issue that relates to much more than selling something. Very simply, everything we say and do communicates what we consider to be important, and what congregations communicate about faith values shapes the way members act on their faith. Therefore, from time to time, congregations need to stop and evaluate what they are communicating. Congregational leaders will likely choose not to use certain forms of communication that don't fit the ethos of that congregation.

Myth 7

Our congregational values are being communicated effectively through words. Our pastor and leaders preach the sermons and put a lot of thought into the words used in our newsletter and on our website.
People are increasingly influenced by images as well as by words. According to communication research, the images projected on a screen during worship and the images used in newsletters and on websites often have as much or more impact that the words associated with them. Much of Jewish and Christian tradition is strongly word oriented, emphasizing the significance of words over images. With the move away from a word-based to an image-based culture, leaders of congregations need to do some careful thinking about the role of visual communication in our time.

Myth 8

We've got a great web designer and newsletter editor, and our newsletter and website are terrific.
In many congregations, one person creates most of the publications. Often, congregational leaders supply verbal text, but the web designer or newsletter editor decides on the layout, photos, and graphics. In this increasingly visual culture, forms of visual communication such as layout, photos, and graphics need to be evaluated to see if they really do communicate what the congre-

gational leaders desire to communicate, particularly if one person is choosing most of them. I believe that all the new communication technologies have created the necessity for "critical friends," people who understand the importance of the new forms of communication for congregations and, at the same time, are willing to look at those forms with a critical eye. These critical friends pay attention to the congregation's websites, blogs, projection screens, and other forms of communication that have a large visual component to see if the visuals really do harmonize with the words used. They evaluate whether the verbal and visual components together communicate important values about the congregation.

Myth 9

If your heart is in the right place, communication takes care of itself.
I agree that the single most important thing for congregations is to worship and follow God in a way that engages hearts and minds. Without faith as the center of its life, a congregation has nothing to offer its members or the world. Faith values cannot be communicated if no faith values are present. But I do not agree that the result of a vibrant faith is that all communication will automatically be okay. Just as individuals with good intentions can benefit from learning listening skills for their personal relationships and speaking skills for their oral communication, so congregations can benefit from considering the implications of the ways they communicate and what they are communicating. In this age of rapidly proliferating communication technologies, this task of evaluation is even more urgent.

Marketing, for Better and for Worse

With so many new ways to communicate, congregational leaders have fresh options for reaching into their wider communities. The word *marketing* is often used when people inside and outside of congregations begin to discuss the way their communication reaches beyond their own organization, and marketing is a concept and practice that can evoke strong emotions.

What exactly is marketing? If you put a dozen people together in a room and ask them to come up with a definition of marketing, you are likely to get a dozen—or more—definitions. Some definitions might describe marketing as brazen and manipulative, the product of a consumer culture gone mad. Others might portray it as a necessary evil. Some definitions would probably describe marketing as a tool that can be used in good or bad ways. If there are Christians present among the dozen people trying to define the word, some of them would probably equate marketing with evangelism, and other Christians would probably strenuously resist equating the two. Some of the Christians in the group might say that marketing is essential for congregations, and others would probably say marketing has come and gone as an important congregational strategy. A few might say that marketing only encourages people to be self-centered consumers and that Christians should not participate in it.

Rather than enter into an extended discussion about the pros and cons of these diverse perspectives, I propose this simple definition of marketing in a congregational context: marketing is reaching out with the purpose of making known that a congregation welcomes new people. Some Christians are comfortable talking about evangelism as an important form of reaching out; others might view marketing as letting newcomers in the community and people in transition, such as new parents, know that the congregation would be delighted to welcome them into the faith community.

Marketing—in the sense of letting people in the community know that the congregation welcomes new people—is something that most congregations do in a variety of ways, such as outdoor signs, announcements in the local newspaper about upcoming events, participation in community events, and hosting community groups like Alcoholics Anonymous. In addition, many congregations take part in outreach ministries such as food banks, community dinners, service projects in the neighborhood, and

CONGREGATIONAL IDENTITY LIBERATES

"When we agree on who we really are, we will make better decisions about what to do. Clergy and lay leaders who know their
congregation's deep identity are able to help the people let go
of false identity and face their reality with courage. A clear and
clearly articulated sense of identity does not prevent change as
one might think. A strong sense of identity empowers the congregation to change. They are liberated by the sense of knowing
who they are as they move into the future."

(Janet R. Cawley, *Who Is Our Church? Imagining Congregational Identity*
[Herndon, VA: The Alban Institute, 2006], 8.)

involvement at local schools. And in this age of digital communication, new forms of outreach are available, including websites,
blogs, and social networking websites. All of these forms of outreach have a component of marketing, because they let people
know the congregation welcomes new people, and all these forms
of outreach are essential and valuable.

These days, a newcomer moving into a community is not likely
to choose a congregation simply because it is affiliated with a denomination or group that is familiar to that newcomer. A couple
who has just had a child and wants to raise that child in a faith
community won't necessarily choose a congregation affiliated
with their childhood faith. All congregations need to pay some
attention to marketing—letting people know the congregation
welcomes new people—even if it is not their favorite activity.

Some congregations have a passion for reaching out into their
communities and welcoming people into their community of
faith. They are deeply committed to marketing and use the word
comfortably. In order to do that well, they need to consider the

ways their values and identity are revealed through their communication, actions, and symbols. They may consider that these values come entirely from their faith and not from the unique characteristics of their congregation, but they still need to evaluate the ways their values are communicated.

Other congregational leaders may not want to engage in marketing because it makes them uneasy for a variety of reasons. I hope that my gentle definition above will make the idea of marketing more attractive to them. I hope that they will also see that the issues of identity and values are significant for people both within and outside a congregation.

Conveying a congregation's identity and values clearly and through a variety of means of communication will help the congregation market itself to the community around it. Clear expressions of values and identity will also have a deep impact on people within the congregation. People already involved in a congregation are shaped by what they hear about that congregation. Their expectations for the life of faith and for their involvement in the community are influenced by the ways the congregation talks about itself and its values.

Some of the people influenced by a congregation's messages regarding identity and values are the ones already in the pews but not particularly engaged with the congregation and its ministries. Perhaps they moved to the area recently and are relatively new to the congregation. Perhaps their schedule is so busy that they attend services only monthly. People who are loosely affiliated with congregations may increase or decrease their commitment at any time. For such people, the communication of a congregation's heart and soul, its DNA, will influence their decisions about commitment.

The congregation's leaders may be deeply committed to spiritual practices that nurture their life of faith in significant ways. But if those practices are not communicated well to the congregation, the people who are on the fringes will never know how much they might benefit from adopting those practices for themselves. The congregation's leaders may be committed to helping every

HONORING PEOPLE WITH DISABILITIES

The way a congregation includes people with disabilities communicates a great deal about its values. Here is a list of suggestions from a Salvation Army minister with a visual disability:

- Print of few copies of the weekly bulletin in a larger font.
- Provide hearing enhancements, called "hearing loops."
- Give opportunities for people with disabilities to lead in worship and use technology to assist. For example, a person with a speech impediment can be invited to read the Scripture and the passage can be shown on the screen behind the person or printed in the bulletin.
- Learn how to say hello in sign language.
- Be aware that a visually impaired person will not see a hand extended. A visually impaired person can be greeted with a touch on the upper arm, the safest place to touch anyone.
- Offset one pew so that people in wheelchairs can fit there.
- Appoint someone as a facilitator of resources for people with disabilities. Some disabilities are invisible, such as early onset arthritis and multiple sclerosis, but adaptations of common congregational practices can still be helpful to people with invisible disabilities.

These practices communicate values of inclusion and welcome to the whole congregation, not only to people with disabilities.

member engage in ministry in a way that uses their gifts, but if that commitment is not communicated well, infrequent attenders might remain totally unaware of the benefits of service.

Long-term attenders are also on a faith journey that is lived out in community. The values and identity of that community will shape the direction of that faith journey. If those values and the congregation's identity are communicated poorly, everyone's growth in faith is compromised.

I had the privilege of serving as an associate pastor in a congregation that I would describe as extremely healthy. Its values were communicated clearly and consistently through sermons and worship style. Its ministries communicated the same values clearly and included thriving programs for children and youth, adult education, small groups, and outreach both locally and internationally. It was a congregation that set a high priority on deep Christian commitment—characterized by prayer, Bible study, and personal commitment to Christian service—lived out in caring community, and this strategy was also communicated clearly.

I left that congregation several years ago and now live many miles away. Recently, a young woman in the congregation was diagnosed with a brain tumor, and I was included in the flurry of e-mails that were sent out recounting her diagnosis, surgery, and recovery. For two days before the surgery, people signed up to pray in half-hourly segments so that someone was praying for her continually for the forty-eight hours before the surgery. After the surgery, people brought meals to her family, and daily e-mail updates were sent out for a couple of weeks so people would know exactly how to pray for her.

As I read those e-mails from a distance, I rejoiced at the way the people involved in caring for her were acting on their faith. The high priority the congregation puts on prayer and on showing love in community were very real in the e-mails. The values promoted consistently in that congregation had deeply influenced the people who were caring for the woman. And the e-mails made clear that the woman herself was growing in trusting God through the whole experience.

As far as I can tell from the e-mails I received from numerous people, the enthusiastic engagement in prayer for this woman and service for her family played a role in nurturing the faith of the people who prayed and served as well as the faith of the woman and her family. This swift response came from the way faith values had been expressed by this congregation over time. Those values were expressed consistently in words and actions, in worship services and in programs. I was involved in helping to create the publications for that congregation for seven years, so I hope those values were expressed just as consistently in the brochures, newsletters, bulletins, and website.

One More Myth

An additional myth about congregational identity needs to be considered. It goes like this: *Part of the congregational leaders' job is to figure out the precise identity of their congregation so that they can describe it concisely in the congregation's mission statement and in its publications.* This myth is grounded in the notion that communication reflects reality. Research shows that communication not only reflects reality but also shapes it. What we say and how we say it influences the way we think about and perceive the world. What we hear, read, and see shapes our perceptions and thoughts as well. We are profoundly shaped by words and visuals and the way they are put together.

The way an issue is framed both verbally and visually can cause a person to see something in a completely new light. This happens in big ways in those "aha" moments that we have all experienced, when something unexpected becomes wonderfully clear. Advertising research shows that seeing something differently happens in a number of small and unconscious ways as well. Images have particular impact in shaping the ways we view reality.

The implications for congregational identity are significant: what congregations communicate about their values and identity—both verbally and visually—not only reflects who they are but also shapes who they are and who they are becoming. What is communicated will shape the way the congregation is perceived by people both within and without. Congregations whose communication and actions emphasize friendliness, outreach, or ministry with children are likely to think about themselves as friendly and engaged with outreach or focused on children, and those attributes are also more likely to be perceived by outsiders.

The members of the congregation where I served as associate pastor were shaped by a variety of messages that stressed that this congregation is a place where people pray for each other and reach out with practical help, particularly in times of great need. Yes, it is a congregation with those characteristics, but it is also a congregation growing into those characteristics as it is shaped by the way it hears and sees itself described.

This myth that communication simply reflects reality is also rooted in the idea that an identity of each congregation can be easily discerned and then described clearly in a few words. I am quite sure that God sees each congregation clearly and precisely, but for those of us on earth, a congregation's identity is made up of many components of its life. Each person in a congregation will have a different sense of what the heart of the congregation is, its central essence. For one person, it might be the small group members with whom they have bonded. For others, the center of the life of the congregation might be the worship music, the sermon, the food bank housed in the basement, or the mission trips to Central America each winter.

A congregation is made of all these aspects and more. All the features of congregational life, all the ministries and activities, reflect the congregation's values and identity, its heart and soul. The challenge is to be intentional in reflecting those values in communication, activities and symbols, emphasizing both the congregation's unity and its diversity.

A comparison of congregational identity to expressions of personal identity today sheds some light on how this process works. People today have begun to express their identities on

BRICOLAGE

Bricolage is a French word used in numerous disciplines to refer to a process of creating by using various things that happen to be available, something like patchworking. Bricolage can also refer to the object that is created. The root meaning of the French word is to fiddle or tinker, and it has come to mean making creative use of materials at hand, whatever their original purpose was.

Communication scholars use the concept of bricolage to discuss websites, particularly personal web pages, blogs, and expressions of personal identity on such websites as Facebook and MySpace. An individual who creates a personal website or a blog will usually adopt, adapt, or refer to a variety of borrowed materials, such as audio or video downloads, quotations and photos from other websites, and links to other websites. These materials will be arranged on the web page in a way that is significant to the person creating the page.

This variety of patchworked materials contributes to the way the reader understands the identity of the person creating the web page, and so the bricolage reflects the identity of the person who assembled the elements. However, the significance of this process goes beyond bricolage as a reflection of the person's identity. The process of bricolage helps a person discover his or her identity, and in some cases the process of assembling the diverse elements actually transforms a person's identity.

Congregational communications, particularly congregational websites, function this way. As photos, graphics, links, audio and video sermons, invitations to events, descriptions of mission activities, statements of purpose, and other items are assembled for a congregational website, a new understanding of the congregation's identity can emerge. This new understanding of who the congregation is and what it is about can become clearer to the people creating the website and also to the people who are viewing the site. Congregational leaders are often confident that their publications reflect the congregation's values and priorities, and they often ignore the possibility that the assembling of the elements for publications, and the arrangement of those elements, actually helps create the congregation's identity.

personal web pages, blogs, and social networking websites such as Facebook and MySpace. Their personal identities are constructed through an assemblage of photos, links to favorite websites, names of online groups they belong to, movie and TV reviews, lists of favorite musicians and songs, books and book reviews, places where they have traveled, quizzes about TV and movie characters they identify with, and interviews about things they like. All of these components speak about who a person is.

Communication scholars argue that identity is constructed. This includes personal identity as well as the identity of organizations such as congregations. Congregations reflect who they are through everything they do and say, but these aspects of congregational life play a role in constructing identity as well as reflecting it.

One of the wonderful characteristics of human beings is that we can change our perspective on things. Sometimes that change of perspective comes fairly easily, particularly when our underlying presuppositions are brought out into the open and when alternative viewpoints make sense and seem appropriate for our time and setting. I hope that reading about the myths in this chapter will help you explore them. And I hope that the remainder of the book will present new and compelling ways of considering the significance of congregational communication around identity and values.

Questions for Reflection, Journaling, and Discussion

1. Do you see any of the myths at work in your congregation? If so, where do you see them? What does your congregation gain by embracing the myths? In what ways do the myths impede effective communication?
2. Which communication technologies does your congregation use well? Describe what makes them effective.
3. Which communication technologies does your congregation use poorly or not at all? What are the factors that

contribute to their lack of effective use? What benefits might the congregation gain from using them more effectively? What might be the costs associated with working on using them more wisely?

4. How would you define marketing? What emotions do you feel when you think about a congregation's need to market itself? In what ways do you see marketing as connected to biblical values?

3 | Communication for Postmodern Pilgrims

IN CHAPTER 1, I DESCRIBED MY OWN JOURNEY navigating the shifts occurring in congregational priorities and in communication practices. Among the many observers who have documented and described these shifts is writer Leonard Sweet, who has analyzed and described the intersection of contemporary culture with faith practices. His description of the characteristics of effective ministry today provides a framework for examining various forms of communication that can help congregational leaders set aside the myths that sometimes cloud our thinking.

Sweet uses the acronym EPIC to describe four characteristics of worship and ministry that meet the needs of people in the post-modern world: experiential, participatory, image driven, and connected.[1] Effective worship and ministry in our time is *experiential*; the senses as well as the mind are engaged through changes in body posture, touch, smell, and taste; and people are encouraged to *experience* the presence of God, not simply talk about it. People can *participate* in a variety of ways in worship and in ministry—by drawing, writing, talking, serving in the inner city, and going on mission trips. *Images* on paper, on projection screens, on walls, and even on clothing are used to communicate truths and stories and to enable engagement. Relational *connections* between people are facilitated and encouraged in the congregation, in homes, in neighborhoods, in workplaces, and online.

When *Post-Modern Pilgrims*, Sweet's book explaining these four characteristics, came out in 2000, I was serving as an associate pastor in a congregation in which the majority of the adults were in their twenties and thirties. The younger congregation members were actively involved in intentional community, a growing arts ministry, contemplative prayer events, and inner city outreach. The congregation had participatory prayer times in worship, a soup and bread lunch after worship once a month, and lots of mission trips and mission opportunities.

Many of the popular activities in the church where I served had more than one of Sweet's EPIC characteristics. The ideas Sweet laid out helped me understand why our congregation appealed to younger people, and I have found his characteristics helpful as lenses for evaluating various aspects of congregational life.

Three of these four characteristics—experiential, participatory, and connected—are related to values long held by people of faith, even if some congregations may not have done a good job of acting on those values. For centuries, saints have desired the *experience* of God's love and care, not just cognitive knowledge of it. The Hebrew Scriptures and the New Testament encourage *participation* and faithfulness in actions. "You are my friends if you do what I command you," Jesus said (John 15:14). Jesus values the one who "hears my words, and acts on them" (Luke 6:47). *Connections* between people—love, care, acts of service, and prayer and worship together—are hallmarks of both Judaism and Christianity. The statement in Micah 6:8 describing what is good—"to do justice, and to love kindness, and to walk humbly with your God"—speaks of experience, participation, and connections.

In our time, a commitment to those three values takes congregations in new directions. Many of the recent options for communication open fresh ways to act on these three values, but the values themselves are not new.

With respect to being image driven, Christians and Jews have a mixed history in the area of visual communication. For many people of faith, the rise in visual culture is one of the distinct challenges for our time, and this chapter will explore some of implications of that shift. First, however, I will analyze new communication technologies common in congregations using as a lens

KINESTHETIC LEARNING

More businesses and educational institutions are paying attention to learning styles as understanding the significance of oral, visual, and kinesthetic learning grows. Churches and synagogues have traditionally relied on oral teaching and communication. Kinesthetic learning overlaps with participatory aspects of congregational life, but kinesthetic learning focuses more narrowly on engaging the physical body.

I can remember the exact moment I realized that younger generations approach their faith in a more kinesthetic fashion than my generation. I was leading a small, intimate worship service at a women's retreat about ten years ago. As I pronounced the benediction, I noticed that several of the younger women cupped their hands as if they wanted to catch God's blessing as I pronounced it.

Congregations that serve younger generations are increasingly using worship stations where people can participate in an activity. Even traditional congregations can make a way for worshipers to bring something forward during worship or use their hands to receive a blessing, draw a simple picture, or write a few words as they sit in the pews. Many Protestant congregations are increasing the frequency of Holy Communion. Focusing on the concept of kinesthetic learning may open up new ways to create participatory activities.

Some forms of kinesthetic participation have visual components to them. I recently attended a worship service in which the sermon focused on Jesus's healing of a blind man. The worship bulletins included black strips of cloth. The black cloths spoke to me of the darkness of spiritual or physical blindness. After the sermon, worshipers were invited to use the cloths as blindfolds during the prayer of confession, and then remove them after receiving forgiveness.

Sweet's four characteristics of effective ministry in postmodern times.

The four characteristics are helpful in understanding the attraction of the new forms of communication for younger generations. Many activities of everyday life today are more experiential, participatory, image driven, and connected, or they manifest those four characteristics in new ways. For example, events that used to be largely passive have become experiential and participatory as people use their cell phones to take pictures and e-mail them to friends or send text messages during the event. Websites, blogs, and online groups invite responses. Television is moving from tightly scripted sitcoms to audience participation in reality TV shows.

Cell phones offer the opportunity to be connected in new ways and in new settings. I have watched my sons, both in their twenties, use cell phones to arrange last-minute connections with groups of friends. I once sat across a restaurant from two people who were sharing a table but each talking on his cell phone. I had to laugh, because I was at that restaurant to have a conversation with my dinner partner. The two people across the room from me were experiencing relational connections as well, but they were relating to people who were not present in the restaurant.

Shopping has become more experiential. Bookstores often now have coffee shops with comfortable armchairs for relaxing and musicians playing live music. Malls, department stores, and specialty stores try to create a pleasant and memorable shopping experience. Online shopping has become more experiential and participatory with the excitement of bidding on items at sites such as eBay.

And images are everywhere. Digital cameras and cell phones with cameras have created the possibility of disseminating photos instantly. Visual communication is increasingly a part of daily life and is closely connected to experiences, participation, and connections with others. In our time, connections have become rapid, frequent, and informal with cell phones, e-mails, and instant messaging, and these forms of communication increasingly have a visual component.

A glance at the common features of websites shows that many have characteristics connected with Sweet's EPIC acronym. New communication technologies intersect with contemporary cultural values as well as values long held by faith communities.

Websites—Participatory and Usually Image Driven

Websites are built on hyperlinks that enable the viewer to navigate to other pages within the website or to pages on a different website. These navigational choices bear some resemblance to thumbing through a magazine. A reader can glance through a magazine and choose which pages to look at. Links on the home page of a website take the viewer to web pages that have been designed to be read in any sequence. In that sense, links on a home page resemble the table of contents of a magazine.

Links on websites, however, have qualities that are quite different from magazines. Each link—whether an inlink to a page on the same website or an outlink to a page on another website—takes the viewer to a new web page that usually has its own set of links.

Each web page, then, as the equivalent of a magazine table of contents, offers an array of choices. Because viewers make their own set of choices, each person's pathway through the website is different. Each person also makes the decision to leave the website and navigate to another site in a unique way. This unique path that each individual creates by moving from one web page to another demonstrates the participatory aspect of websites, a new communication phenomenon. Note the contrast with television, which is watched in a much more passive fashion.

Websites are also usually image driven. Photos and graphics can be easily added to websites, and a website without any photos or graphics would usually not attract many viewers. In addition,

FACEBOOK, MYSPACE, FRIENDSTER, AND BEBO

*Experiential, participatory,
image driven, connected*

Social networking websites are powerful examples of the attraction of EPIC characteristics for younger generations. In addition, they exemplify the significance of creating an online identity, which parallels creating identity on congregational websites.

Participants on social networking websites create an online profile—or identity—using photos, quizzes, travelogues of trips taken, book and movie reviews, favorite TV shows and characters, links to film clips, personal histories, comparisons with famous people, descriptions of moods, song dedications, description of their job, and discussion of topics. Participants can participate in groups and identify networks they belong to. They can list their friends, and they can make connections with mutual friends of their friends. Their friends can contribute to the creation of their online identity by commenting on various portions of their profile.

They stay connected to their friends because they get automatic updates every time friends post something new to their profiles. Many people who use social networking websites say that the websites have helped them nurture relationships.

Values are expressed through links, reviews, activities, and discussions. The construction of identity on social networking websites is playful, multifaceted, visual, and always changing. "Who am I?" takes on new forms in electronic media, but similarities to the construction of real life identity abound.

websites are visual in a way that goes beyond photos and graphics. Fonts, colors, and layout contribute to the sense of a website as a visual object, even when few photos and graphics are used.

Basic website features make almost all websites participatory and image driven. A number of optional features of websites make them experiential and connected as well.

Podcasts and Streaming Audio—Experiential

Downloading a sermon or an address and listening to it on an iPod or listening to a sermon online is different from reading the text of that sermon, in the same way that hearing authors talk on a radio show is different from reading articles or books they have written. Tone of voice and word emphasis is different when we hear it than when we read it. For most people, hearing someone's voice has an experiential component.

Video Downloads and Streaming Video—Experiential and Image Driven

Some congregations with large budgets have videos on their home pages to introduce newcomers to the congregation or to advertise an upcoming event. Some congregations videotape their sermons and offer them on their websites. Downloading video or watching it online is experiential, like listening to podcasts and streaming audio but with images added. Other congregations use video downloads or streaming video for sermons, and some congregational websites use videos on the home page as a way to represent something about the congregation's life and to engage website viewers.

Online Quizzes—Participatory and Connected

Online quizzes are becoming more common on many kinds of websites. Some congregations use quizzes on their home pages to ask questions about the congregation's life, reactions to the website, or a question related to faith. When website viewers consider the question and make their choice of response, they are participating. The responses of other viewers often appear on the screen, creating a feeling of connection to those other viewers.

Links to Movie Clips or YouTube Clips— Experiential, Participatory, Image Driven, and Connected

Links to video clips of interesting speakers, amusing events, and even unusual advertisements are increasingly common on websites, particularly on blogs. The engagement of the senses—hearing as well as seeing—contributes to making these clips experiential. They are image driven like all video downloads and streaming video. On YouTube, they become participatory because the viewer is asked to rate the video after it plays and to comment on it. Because the ratings and comments reflect other people's opinions, viewers feel some degree of connection with others who have viewed the same clip. Some congregations provide links on their websites to movie clips or YouTube clips that illustrate a sermon theme or something connected to the congregation's life.

Blogs—Can Be Participatory, Image Driven, and Connected

In format, blogs can range from text-based online diaries to complex websites with photos, images, and varied layouts. In their most text-based form, with no links or options for feedback, blogs are similar to magazines or newspapers but written in a format more like a diary. In their more complex form, with links, photos or graphics, and options for feedback, they are participatory and image driven. They can nurture moderately significant connections if viewers engage in dialogue with each other or with the blog writer. Blogs associated with congregations are becoming more common. Some congregational leaders have created blogs as a forum to talk frequently about issues related to the life of the congregation. Some congregations provide links to blogs by well-known people.

Online Groups—Can Be Participatory, Image Driven, and Connected

If you want to find people who share your last name, who have experienced the same kind of cancer, or who have adopted a child from Guatemala, an online group undoubtedly exists to help you make that connection. Online groups provide opportunity for connection between people who have almost anything in common. Sometimes members of online groups post photos, and in that case the groups are image driven. Online groups become participatory when the viewer decides to write a response rather than simply reading what others have written. The degree of connection varies, but some members of online groups develop such intimate connections that they fly across the country to meet people face-to-face whom they met first in an online group focused on a topic of mutual interest.

Search Engines—Participatory

Do you want to find the web page that describes the congregation's preschool room or the upcoming outreach trip? Some congregations offer a search option on their websites, and searching is a way of encouraging participation, because the viewer chooses what to search for and how to respond to the results of the search.

I have listed these website features not because I think each congregation should have them all on its website, but because I want to model the kind of assessment that helps congregational leaders understand the appeal of new communication technologies to younger generations. Because new communication technologies emerge continuously, this brief assessment can provide a framework for evaluating new communication technologies as they appear.

Of the four characteristics that make up the EPIC acronym, "image driven" is usually the most challenging for leaders of congregations. Wise engagement with visual communication will probably be a significant part of the learning curve for congregational leaders in the years to come.

Our Image-Driven Culture

In the second half of the twentieth century, the advertising industry discovered the power of images to persuade people to buy things. Images give information about products, but their power goes far beyond information. Images evoke distant places, tap into a variety of desires, and make connections between products and values. Images make arguments. In advertising, they are designed to convince the viewer of the value of a product.

A magazine advertisement for a resort in Florida shows a man and woman embracing beside a huge empty swimming pool with a deserted beach in the background. The rich colors of sunset fill the sky behind them, and the scene is beautiful and inviting. The ad evokes sexual and relational intimacy. It taps into desires for beauty and uncrowded spaces. It speaks of luxury: the luxury of time away from responsibilities and the luxury of wealth. The advertisement, because it is strategic and well designed, creates longing and desire in many viewers. It makes the argument that choosing to go to that particular resort will result in some wonderful outcomes.

People in the advertising industry might say that the longing was there all along, and a well-chosen photograph simply brings it to the surface and associates that longing with a particular product, in this case a specific resort in Florida. What could be wrong with that?

People who are skeptics about consumer culture might respond that the image is manipulative. No resort, no matter how luxurious, offers a swimming pool and beach where two people can be completely alone. The photo implies that relational intimacy will be certainly found at that resort, which is ridiculous. And the advertisement validates a love of luxury on a planet where more than twenty thousand people die each day from the effects of poverty.

Most days our eyes land on hundreds of advertising images, and we have little awareness of the effect of those images on us. So much of what happens when we see an image is unconscious. Can images be used wisely to nurture faith?

Some communities of faith have enthusiastically embraced images as a way to communicate values associated with their faith. They project images on screens in worship and publish photos in newsletters and on websites. They offer downloadable or streaming video sermons. Other congregations may have a few banners but they haven't embraced the visual culture profoundly, sometimes because of financial considerations or lack of resources. Some people feel vaguely uneasy with the rise of visual culture, while others are negative about the consumerism inherent in the way images are used in many settings.

Also noteworthy is that advertisements don't have a chance of closing the deal—for example, getting people to sign up for a vacation at that particular resort—unless the words accompanying the advertisement are extremely well chosen. The advertising industry has majored in setting the mood through its use of enticing images, but advertisers have been weaker at clear communication of the concrete actions they want people to take. People in the direct marketing industry still believe that "copy is king," because words give the specific instructions that motivate people to act in a particular way. Words, often supported by images, have the most impact in everyday persuasion.

The direct marketing perspective lays out a practical argument about the importance of words. In addition, theological concerns have been expressed by some Christian scholars and observers who are deeply troubled by the increasing use of images in the postmodern world. They stress that the Judeo-Christian heritage has often been centered on words, in contrast with paganism, which has been more dependent on images. They note that the decline in the Christian faith in Western Europe in the Middle Ages, which preceded the Reformation, was caused at least in part by the church's assimilation of pagan forms and images.[2] A quick look at the history of the use of images in faith communities will give background and context for this issue.

A Brief History of Images and Faith

The role of images in the life of faith has been controversial in many places and times. Two major disputes among Christians about images went on for decades and gave birth to the term *iconoclasm*, which means the breaking of images.

The first controversy, in the seventh and eighth centuries, involved a conflict between the church of the West, centered in Rome, and the church in the East, centered in Constantinople. This first dispute was precipitated by a number of factors, including the role of relics, superstition associated with icons, and the strong emphasis put on the verbal text by Christians in the West. The church in the West argued that Christians should stand with Jews and Muslims in affirming the significance of the second commandment (Exod. 20:4), which forbids the creation of graven images because they can become idols that are worshiped in the place of the true God.

Over the course of two centuries of debate, numerous arguments were advanced. One point made by Christians in the East was that the images forbidden in the second commandment were *graven* images, which they took to mean three-dimensional artlike statues. The art used in worship in the East was two-dimensional, and although Christians in the East agreed that the danger of idol worship was important, they believed another danger was inherent in doing away with all images. Without pictures of Jesus and the saints, people might come to believe that Jesus did not really take on human flesh, which would profoundly alter the nature of the Christian faith. And without pictures, the saints might be viewed as so otherworldly they would not function as models for Christians to follow.

After decades of controversy and debate, the Eastern Church continued to create images and use them in worship, although the characteristics of the images changed to some extent after that first iconoclastic controversy. These controversies laid some of the groundwork for the split between the Eastern Church and Western Church in 1054.

In the medieval period, the church in the West rediscovered the helpfulness of images as a way to communicate religious truth in a time before widespread literacy. Bible stories were illustrated in stained glass windows for the benefit of people who couldn't read and wouldn't have access to a Bible even if they knew how to read it. Statues of Mary and the saints were viewed at least in part as educational, providing an opportunity for people to remember the story of the saint's life when they saw the statue. The stations of the cross were introduced as a way for Christians to journey with Jesus to the cross without visiting the Holy Land. Even the architecture of churches was viewed as a way to communicate God's transcendence and immanence.

A second period of controversy about images arose at the time of the Reformation in the sixteenth and seventeenth centuries. Most of the reformers believed that images and statues had become objects of worship in the medieval church, and so they purposely emphasized words over images. Some reformers spoke strongly against images.

This movement, again called iconoclasm, shaped the next four centuries of Protestant life in many settings. Most Protestant churches emphasized music as the most important expression of creativity in the churches. Often theater was also acceptable because it is largely word-based. But in many Protestant churches, visual art was viewed as extraneous or even damaging to faith.

The history of Jewish use of images is also noteworthy. Throughout most of Jewish history, the second commandment was interpreted by rabbinic scholars to mean that much visual art was forbidden, particularly the portrayal of human beings. As with Protestant Christians, music and theater were major artistic expressions for Jews. In addition, a tradition of textual art arose in the Middle Ages, and Jewish texts were adorned with beautiful illuminations.

In Europe during and after the Middle Ages, Jews were subjected to countless forms of restriction and were not allowed the rights of citizenship. One restriction was that Jews were forbidden to engage in the visual arts as a profession. This changed at the time of the Emancipation when discriminatory laws against Jews were abolished and Jews were granted citizenship and allowed to participate fully in society.

The Emancipation occurred in European countries at different times, beginning with France in the late 1700s and continuing in other countries throughout the nineteenth century. After Emancipation and the huge changes it brought to daily life, Jews began to participate in the visual arts, and many famous artists of the twentieth century were Jewish, such as Marc Chagall, Camille Pissarro, and Mark Rothko.

Another significant aspect of the history of images is quite unrelated to the life of faith. For most of human history images were relatively rare because they could not be reproduced easily. In many settings, people had to enter sacred caves, churches, or the home of a wealthy person in order to see many images. Twentieth-century technology made possible the proliferation of images. Electricity and modern chemicals are required to print color photos in magazines and newspapers. Electricity runs movie projectors, televisions, and computers. The plethora of images that shape our everyday lives could only have happened in the last fifty to seventy-five years with the rise in cheap and readily available electricity and other technological tools.

The Implications of This History

Much of the debate in Christian churches about images centered on the role of images in worship. An extensive literature explores the theological implications of images of God, Jesus, the saints, and biblical stories, particularly addressing the appropriateness of using such images in worship. By and large, this literature doesn't explore the significance of other kinds of images for other purposes, and much of this literature is in the Eastern Orthodox, Roman Catholic, and Anglican traditions, where images were discussed more widely than in Protestant traditions.

The fact that many Protestants and Jews have discouraged the use of images for much of their history has implications for understanding visual culture today. Many leaders of congregations in those traditions stand in a long heritage of disregard for the visual arts and visual communication. Protestant congregational leaders can draw on centuries of theological reflection on music, drama, and verbal arts like poetry, but not the visual arts.

Further, the relative paucity of images in everyday life until the last half century means that reflection on visual communication outside worship is a new phenomenon. People today have almost no heritage of reflection on what might be called secular images, and particularly on the ways images from the wider culture might be used strategically in marketing congregations or communicating faith values. Theological reflection on visual communication as it is used today is in its infancy.

Some congregations have dived into the use of projection screens during worship, visual arts ministries, and highly visual websites that sometimes look like secular advertisements. On the one hand, they are doing the right thing in order to reach out to younger generations. On the other hand, the lack of theological reflection is troubling.

How do images work? How do they connect to emotions and values? How do they make arguments? People of faith are committed to communicating God's truth; in what ways do images do that well and in what ways do they do it poorly? In what ways can images communicate God's love? The peace of Christ? A call to holy and obedient living?

People are able to process visual information much more quickly than verbal information. One study indicated that we process images sixty thousand times faster than words.[3] If this research is accurate, what are the implications?

Leonard Sweet calls our culture "imageholic."[4] Is there a danger inherent in the use of all images? Is the viewer encouraged into addiction rather than thoughtful engagement with faith? Do certain kinds of images, because of their frequent use in advertising, evoke consumerism and consumption?

I can give a brief initial answer to some of these questions, but much additional reflection is needed. I believe it will take decades before people of faith develop theological competence in assessing visual communication and in using it wisely to evoke values that come from faith.

Images at Work

How do images get our attention and communicate messages to us? Imagine for a moment that you are going on vacation in a few weeks, and you want to find a congregation to visit while you are away. You find a list of congregations on the web page of the city where you are going, and you click on the links to the various congregations' websites. You look at several websites, trying to get the flavor of the congregations to decide if you want to visit.

On your fifth or sixth try, a very appealing website downloads onto your screen. A group of four photos front and center on the home page captures your attention: a cityscape with a gold sky, a man holding a young child, two women and two teenagers in hard hats on a construction site, and a group of people in a worship service playing tambourines and maracas.

You find yourself focusing on these photos. It seems likely to you that the photo of the city, gilded with golden light, is saying that this congregation is involved with its city and sees the good in its community. The photo of the man with the child and the teenagers with the women on the construction site seem to indicate a commitment to children and youth as well as an intergenerational approach and a commitment to community service. The fact that the people in the worship service are playing percussion instruments indicates worship may be participatory.

Why are these particular photos more engaging than the photos you saw on the other websites? Are they simply better photos? Is the attraction related to you and your particular values, concerns, and history? Do you have a love of your own city, a brother with a small child, a teenager you hope will get involved in community service, or a fondness for playing tambourines? Or are these photos iconic in some way, tapping into the values and stories of many or even most people?

Images work in part because they are polyvalent; they can have numerous meanings. The gilded cityscape could indicate a concern for the needs of the city, an overly idealized view of the city, or a hope for the future of the city. The man and small child could be a father and son, a volunteer in a Sunday school class and a pupil, or an uncle and nephew.

As we process images, we come to a conclusion about what we think an image represents. That expenditure of energy, as we wrestle briefly with possible meanings and settle on one, impresses the image in our mind. This is part of the reason images are memorable.

In addition, images connect us with metaphors. The word *metaphor* comes from the Greek word for transport, and the basic idea of a metaphor involves the transport of an idea from one word or phrase to another. The metaphor of the light shining in darkness has great power in the life of faith: God's goodness and love, represented by the light, shines into human pain and sorrow, represented by darkness.

A photo of a candle in a dark space functions in the same way that a verbal metaphor does. Perhaps the candle is held in a child's small hand, evoking purity and innocence. Perhaps the child and the candle are clearly in a congregational setting, indicating that this congregation is a place where people can experience God's light in a pure and innocent setting, apart from the darkness of human evil and pain.

ONE CONGREGATION'S PHOTOS

One congregation's embrace of the visual culture is attractive and appealing. Throughout the interior halls and walls of the church building a couple dozen framed photographs of the congregation in action are hanging. The photos are large, about two feet wide by three feet tall, and they show children doing artwork, adults and children engaged in projects together, adults and youth in worship and doing mission. The photos must have been expensive to print and frame, but they have held up well over time. I have visited that church building many times for meetings over the decade the photos have been there, and I never tire of looking at the faces in the photos.

I believe the photos accomplish several things. They promote the idea that congregational life involves attending worship services but goes beyond the worship service. They give visitors a glimpse into the broader life of the congregation, helping newcomers and even regular attenders see the kinds of intergenerational activities and mission projects they might engage in if they became more involved. And because the subject of all the photos is people, they brighten up the dull walls of the church, saying in effect that yes, the walls and the building are here, but people are what really matter to us.

Even seemingly straightforward photos of people can function as metaphors. The photo of a man carrying a small child, when it has a prominent place on a congregational website, can function as an affirmation that this congregation is a place where small children and solo parents are welcome.

However, a photo cannot be expected to evoke the same metaphor for every viewer. The polyvalent nature of photos means that different viewers probably connect the photo with different meanings. Imagine a website viewer who was sexually abused as a child by a man who resembles the man in the photo holding the child. In that case, the photo might transport the concept of sexual abuse from the viewer's past to the congregation represented by the website. Because of this aspect of the polyvalent nature of images, the limits of images in communication must be considered.

Profound Changes

Shane Hipps, the author of *The Hidden Power of Electronic Culture* and a Mennonite minister with a background in advertising, believes that images do not articulate categories or abstractions very well.[5] Hipps points out that images work very differently from words: "A photograph cannot create categories; it just provides an impression of reality. An image shows us the world as an array of ambiguity and mystery. It does not explain or organize the world the way language can. As a result, we become increasingly tolerant of ambiguity and mystery—the very things images can best depict."[6]

Hipps brings a valuable perspective when he argues that images communicate in a way different from words and that images can evoke the mystery of faith and affirm individual experiences of faith. Hipps goes on to argue that the rise of images, both in the wider culture and in faith communities, has brought about significant changes that we are only beginning to realize.

He notes several trends in Protestant Christian communities that he thinks have resulted from an increased use of images: increased appreciation of Jesus's parables in place of the analytical language of the apostle Paul; a higher regard for Eastern Orthodox spiritual practices, which are more closely related to images; as well as a greater respect for medieval Christian spiritual disciplines, which are less analytical and more experiential. Hipps believes that a greater appreciation for the mystery of faith and a greater tolerance for diverse ways of expressing faith may also be connected to the rise in images.

Other experts argue that the rise in visual communication has paralleled and accompanied the shifts that Hipps describes, not necessarily caused them. All of the shifts he mentions, along with the rise in visual communication, seem likely to be manifestations of the decline of the modern period and the rise of postmodernism. Modernism stressed scientific, verifiable truth expressed in analytical statements, while current postmodern culture stresses individual experience lived in relationship and described in stories. And images excel at telling stories.

In our time, visual images are here to stay, visual culture is increasingly significant, and people of faith are only beginning to grapple with the implications. As visual communication becomes more common in diverse areas of life with the proliferation of digital photos and photos and graphics downloaded off the Internet, many congregational ministries will need to consider the ways they will engage in visual communication. An increased engagement with visual arts in congregations is one way congregations are linking the rise in visual culture with faith experience.

God as the First Artist

More congregations are exploring the visual arts as an avenue for faith expression as the power of images becomes more obvious and as images become more central to everyday life. According to Princeton sociologist of religion Robert Wuthnow, congregations have begun experimenting with greater participation in the arts by holding art festivals and craft fairs and by hosting artist-in-residence programs. Wuthnow describes this array of arts activities, including the visual arts, in his book *All in Sync*. In addition, he notes that films, theater productions, popular music, and the visual arts have increasingly explored religious and spiritual issues, showing the close connection possible between the arts and the sacred. Wuthnow believes that "one of the most important reasons that spirituality seems so pervasive in American culture is the publicity it receives because of its presence in the arts."[7]

PRAYING WITH ICONS

Worship in an Eastern Orthodox church is a visual feast. Christians in Orthodox churches have long prayed using icons. They usually have icons in their homes for prayer, and a part of congregational worship involves praying in front of the iconostasis, a wall with numerous icons hung on it.

Icons are sacred images of Jesus, Mary, or the saints or illustrated scenes from biblical stories. Typically they are painted on wood, although other surfaces can be used. One unique characteristic of icons is that there is no visible source of light in the painting. The person pictured in the icon is viewed as being the source of light. Usually the people pictured in icons have extremely large eyes, and praying with icons involves imagining the person in the icon looking at you rather than you looking at the icon. God gazes at us through the enlarged eyes of Jesus or the saint represented in the icon.

In recent years, Protestant and Roman Catholic Christians have discovered the joy of praying with icons. A Roman Catholic church near my former home had a beautiful icon of Jesus, and I used to visit that church regularly to let Jesus in the icon gaze at me. When my husband and I moved away, I got a postcard of that icon. It sits on my desk, and I often pause as I work to let Jesus gaze on me. His gaze is full of acceptance and compassion, yet his eyes also call me to commitment and conviction. I know that my experience of praying with this one icon is probably very limited and rudimentary compared to people who have been praying with icons their whole life long, but I am deeply grateful for the acceptance and compassion from Jesus that I have experienced from that icon. And his loving gaze gives me resolution to continue in the life of faith.

More people of faith are engaging with the visual arts as a pathway to spirituality. Praying with icons is only one way. Congregations are increasingly holding seminars in which artistic expression—making collages, working with clay, even finger painting—functions as a way to express one's spiritual journey. Another pathway involves meditation or journaling focused on works of art. Spiritual disciplines centered on the visual arts will likely become more common and new forms will likely emerge.

Wuthnow describes the growing connection between the arts and faith:

> Churches and synagogues, museums and galleries, and community art programs are playing an increasing role in bringing Americans' interests in the arts to bear on their quests for the sacred. In the process, new attention is being given to the religious imagination, and many people are experimenting with the arts in their devotional lives, at their houses of worship, and in their efforts to serve others. The consequences are sometimes profound. Making greater use of the arts becomes a path to personal growth. For many churches, it has also been a dynamic source of new vitality.[8]

As I studied websites for my dissertation, I came across numerous congregations with artists' galleries on their websites. In one case, it was clear that the art displayed on the site had been displayed earlier on the walls of the church in rotating art displays. Several websites I studied talked about God as "an artistic God," who showed exquisite creativity in the creation of the physical world and calls us to reflect that same kind of creativity in our lives.

Some websites talked at length about the connection between the arts and God's nature. Here is one example:

> God is beautiful and His creation reflects His beauty. God is the ultimate artist. God's beauty can be found in nature. God also created people in His image and likeness as works of beauty. So we are also all creators. When we experience beauty and creativity we connect with God. [In our church we try] to experience beauty through music, images, art, films, candles, and multi-sensory experiences. We value many different forms of creative expression and use a variety of media to convey God's love.[9]

Images on screens, in newsletters, on websites, and in many other settings will play an increasing role in communities of faith, and ongoing theological reflection will be necessary as visual communication continues to proliferate. In the next chapter, this discussion will continue as we consider the role of images on websites.

Questions for Reflection, Journaling, and Discussion

1. Do you agree with Leonard Sweet that ministry in the postmodern period has become more experiential, participatory, image driven, and connected? In what places in congregational life have you seen each of these characteristics? In what ways could your congregation engage more fully with these characteristics?
2. Consider your personal reaction to characteristics of congregational life that are experiential, participatory, image driven, and connected. What do you like about these characteristics? What makes you uncomfortable?
3. What kinds of opportunities do you think the Internet offers congregations? What are you most concerned about?
4. Think about the role of visual images in your own life. What kinds of images have power for you? In what ways have images helped you grow in faith? What do you think is the place of images in the life of faith?
5. Think about the places where your congregation uses images and the places where it does not. What are the pros and cons of your congregation's practices regarding images?

4 | Websites

Our New Front Page

JONATHAN, TWENTY-EIGHT, BELIEVES WEBSITES function like a "front page" for organizations. He notes that his generation surfs the Internet continuously, both during the work day and during leisure hours, and that they would almost never visit a congregation or other organization without first checking out its website.

Whether or not Jonathan can speak for an entire generation, organizational websites are certainly proliferating. More organizations, including congregations, are beginning to see the strategic possibilities websites give them.

Jonathan is my son, and his viewpoint influenced me when I chose the topic for the dissertation I wrote recently for my PhD in communication. I studied websites produced by congregations and interviewed people who create and maintain websites for congregations. I spent my work week for almost two years focused on congregational websites, and I came away convinced that many congregational leaders have a limited view of both the opportunities and challenges presented by websites.

Making Connections

As noted in chapter 3, in some ways websites are like colorful magazines, with words, photos, and graphics communicating a

Parts of this chapter appeared in the article "Our New Front Door: How Congregational Websites Communicate Church Vision," which I wrote for the Alban Institute publication Congregations, *Spring 2008, Number 2.*

message. However, websites have one characteristic that is new to this medium: links from one web page to another. Viewers navigate their way through websites based on their own interests, and they may move to another website because a link takes them there.

In the same way that photos can communicate values in a nonverbal way, links on websites communicate a great deal about the congregation. What aspects of the congregation's life are so significant that they get a prominent link on the home page, a link with bold print or perhaps a graphic? What activities get links on lists, menus, or navigation bars? Which outside organizations does this congregation value highly enough that a link is provided on the home page? Are newcomers appreciated enough that a prominent link is provided with information just for them? Are potential questions significant enough that there is a link to frequently asked questions?

In the research I did for my dissertation, megachurches—obviously successful in drawing in new people—were noteworthy for the kinds of links on their home pages. Many of them had prominent links for newcomers. Often, the link was large, set apart, and asked its particular version of "New to Christ Church?" In other cases, the link was in a menu. These links took the viewer to pages with basic information about the church, such as what to wear, what children and youth can expect, what happens during a typical worship service, and where to park. Sometimes the information was written in a "Frequently Asked Questions" (FAQ) format.

In addition to the links specifically for newcomers, almost all the megachurch sites had numerous links to pages letting people know how they could get involved in small groups, classes, and mission and service opportunities both inside and outside the congregation. They also provided links on their home pages to information about their programs for children and youth.

Other congregations had prominent statements on their home pages that expressed an inclusive welcome, but the megachurches were more likely to act out that welcome by providing links for newcomers and links to a variety of ways to get involved. In fact,

WHY HOME PAGES MATTER

The home page of a congregation's website should be carefully constructed, representing the core values and identity of a congregation as wisely and effectively as possible, using words, photos, and layout strategically. It should also give the practical information (particularly location and worship time) that viewers need. Statistics of website use show why the home page matters so much. Here is a list of the number of hits on one congregation's website in a month:

- Home page—2,112
- Congregational values page—311
- Audio and media page (includes sermon downloads)—232
- How to get involved in ministry page—222
- Marketplace (a place to exchange things and services)—185
- News and events—184
- Pastors and staff—175
- Contact us—121
- Small groups—119

Some home pages are sparse and bare, with little information and only one photo, often a photo of the building. Some are quite unattractive to look at, with a bland layout, poor quality photos, and unharmonious colors. Some are cluttered with too much information and a hodgepodge of fonts, colors, and styles. An attractive home page that presents key information about a congregation's heart and soul is an excellent investment of time, money, and energy.

the megachurches in my sample were less likely to use the word *welcome*. Websites offer a welcome in a variety of ways by wise use of the structure of websites, and using the word *welcome* is only one way to convey a congregation's desire for new people to feel comfortable.

In a similar way, some congregations talked about justice for the poor, but others had links to opportunities to serve the poor, perhaps at a homeless shelter or Habitat for Humanity house. Links to information about activities speak strongly of congregational values, and they also enable people to become connected.

Verbal text, photos, and graphics on the home page can be used as links or to complement links, communicating the value a congregation places on a particular aspect of its communal life. On one church website, the link to information for newcomers was a graphic in the form of a luggage tag, a playful and eye-catching sign that the congregation wants newcomers to be comfortable. Many congregations use photos to accompany prominent links on the home page, such as a photo of a small group placed near a link to small groups. Sometimes statements about the significance a congregation places on a particular ministry accompany a link: "Join us as we reach out into our community to show the love of Christ" or "Spiritual growth and relational connection are priorities for us. Our classes and small groups can help you connect and grow."

Some congregations use links on their home page to other web pages that describe the congregation's history or provide a statement of faith. In both cases, these links speak of congregational values. A number of congregations post statements of faith that are quite long, which appears to indicate that the congregation places a high value on doctrine. One of the websites I studied had numerous web pages about the congregation's history, illustrated with abundant old and fascinating photos. All those web pages communicated intentionally or unintentionally that the congregation valued its history—to the point that, to me, it seemed that it might be stuck in the past.

Links to organizations outside the congregation also communicate significant things about the identity of the congregation, particularly on the home page. Links to denominational agencies convey a commitment to connections within the denomination. Links to community groups convey a commitment to connections within the city or town. Links to local arts groups, the blood bank, or the local Habitat for Humanity project communicate the way the congregation engages in its city or county. Links to national and international organizations also convey values.

Some congregations have a separate page of links to organizations, and these links also convey something about the congregation's priorities. When a congregational website offers few links to denominational resources, community groups, or national and international organizations, it communicates a sense of self-sufficiency and independence. Links to websites beyond the congregation communicate the ways the congregation values being involved in the wider world.

Reaching All Audiences

Congregational websites have three audiences, two of them primary and one of them less prominent. One audience is congregation members. Often they come to the website for information. What time is that missionary speaking tonight? And where? They also visit their congregation's website to download the sermon in audio, video, or written form. Keeping the website updated with factual information and up-to-date sermons is key for this audience.

A second audience is potential visitors. Is the time of the worship service posted on the home page? Is there a link to directions to the church? Is basic information about the congregation presented—both verbally and visually—so that a visitor would have some sense of this congregation's priorities? Are there links with information specifically for newcomers? Or links to general information about the church that newcomers would value?

Some of the potential visitors who look at your congregation's website are like my husband and me after our recent move, committed to finding a congregation. Other potential visitors have been wounded or alienated by their past involvement in their church or synagogue and are looking at congregational websites in a much more tentative fashion. Does the website convey that spiritual seekers are welcome? That questions are valued? That people don't have to be perfect to attend?

Congregational websites often fail to meet the needs of one of these two core audiences, members and potential visitors. A careful audit of the website, evaluating whether the needs of these audiences are addressed, can be helpful in assessing the effectiveness of a website.

A third audience is people from other congregations who are looking for resources. Perhaps someone visits a congregation on vacation, enjoys the sermon, and comes back to that congregation's website each week to read or listen to the sermon. Perhaps a children's ministry leader is looking for new ideas, scanning other churches' websites to get ideas for ways of serving children. A worldwide network of connections is facilitated by the existence of congregational websites, a fascinating new manifestation of the body of Christ and of Jewish solidarity.

The Rise of the Visual

One manifestation of the rise in visual communication in our time is the use of photos and graphics on websites. Websites are an assemblage of words and images, and experts on websites affirm that the visual components have a more immediate impact on viewers than do the verbal components because our brains process images much more quickly than words.

The visual aspects of websites that have immediate impact are twofold: The photos and graphics on a website draw the viewer's attention. In addition, viewers immediately take in the overall arrangement of each web page—the way the verbal text looks and the way the words, graphics, and photos are positioned on the page. Only secondarily do web viewers absorb the content of the words on the page.

RESEARCH ON WEBSITES

In my dissertation research on websites I found several interesting differences between the home pages of congregations. These differences are worthy of discussion as congregational leaders plan or evaluate their websites.

Imperative verbs. Some congregations use many imperative verbs on their home page. "Join us for worship." "Sign up here." "Click here for more information." "Come on a mission trip." "Join a small group." Other congregations use many fewer imperative verbs, giving information about the activities of the congregation in an inviting way but without using such directive and commanding verbs. Imperative verbs can be welcoming. They can also feel pushy and bit overwhelming. They should be used intentionally.

Links to local organizations. Some congregations have links to local community organizations on their home pages, communicating their connection to their town or city, their engagement with the arts, or their commitment to other local endeavors. Other congregations have no links on their home pages to outside organizations, communicating self-sufficiency and perhaps even insularity. On home pages, the presence or absence of links to outside organizations communicates the values of a congregation, whether intentionally or unintentionally.

The arts. Some congregations have clear references and links on their home pages to their programs connected with visual arts, music, drama, and other forms of artistic expression. In our time, when more people connect their spirituality to the arts, a reference on the home page to a congregation's involvement with the arts may be a wise strategic choice.

Openness to questions. Some congregations indicate on their home pages or elsewhere on their websites that they are a place that welcomes people who have questions. This openness to questions may be another strategic choice in our time, when fewer people have a lifelong faith commitment and more people are exploring spiritual options.

Most of the website producers I interviewed for my dissertation affirmed that the pastors and leaders of their congregations are largely word oriented. My interviewees told me that their pastors and other congregational leaders generate announcements of events and descriptions of the church that are usually designed for newsletters, brochures, and printed bulletins. Web designers edit these verbal texts, usually shortening them significantly, and pair them with photos and other images to create a pleasing whole.

Note the disconnect here. Congregational leaders are charged with shepherding the congregation and communicating its vision, yet the aspect of the website that carries the greatest impact—the visual components, such as photos and graphics, as well as the overall visual structure—is usually determined by one person, the web designer. This person is usually a member of the congregation who volunteers to create the site, a paid employee, or a paid independent contractor. In very few cases is the designer a leader of the congregation.

Many congregational websites are quite effective and interesting, but are they communicating the values of the congregation in ways that mesh with the vision for the congregation established by its leaders? Unless leaders of congregations take websites seriously, websites will continue to be the work of one person, or a small number of people, who may or may not be closely connected to the leaders and their vision.

The Right Image

During a recent conversation with an expert in church communication, I asked him what he considered to be the significant mistakes congregations make in their communication. He said the single biggest mistake is to communicate that the church is identified with the building.

Many congregational websites feature a photo of the building at the top of the home page. Often that photo is the only photo on the home page. If a congregation wants to communicate that its values are closely connected to its building, then a photo of the building is perfectly appropriate. However, I imagine that most leaders of congregations would not talk about their building first when they discuss their congregation's values.

A number of congregations use verbal text on their home pages that communicates a strong welcome: a statement that all are invited to attend the congregation and join in its activities. What kinds of photos or graphics best accompany those kinds of statements? A number of congregations use photos of people to communicate welcome.

Scholars who study photographs of people note that photos of a person's upper body or head communicate more intimacy than photos that include the whole body. They also note that people in photos who are looking at the viewer communicate an invitation or demand. This contrasts with photos of people looking away from the camera; these photos communicate an offer, with less demand placed on the viewer. Based on this research, the most invitational—or demanding—photos are those that include the head or upper body, with the person or people in the photographs looking directly at the viewer. The advertising profession has been using photos like this for years.

In all the websites I pored over, I found that photos of people felt more invitational than photos of buildings. Photos of people seemed to be more in harmony with statements of welcome. But there were limits. Some websites had so many photos of people looking into the camera that after a while, those websites felt overwhelming and even pushy, as if too much was being demanded of me. Photos of people involved in congregational activities, not looking into the camera, gave me a window into the congregation's life without demanding anything of me.

This issue of demand versus offer in photos is worthy of discussion. What do you want your website to communicate? That all are welcome? Or that you strongly urge people to attend? Photos contribute to this message.

Groupings of people in photos also communicate the kind of relationships that are valued in a congregation. Photos of people from different generations involved in activities together communicate that the congregation values and nurtures intergenerational activities. A preponderance of photos that appear to be traditional nuclear families indicates that nontraditional families may not be welcome. Photos of groups of people who appear to be from various ethnic backgrounds communicate an openness to diverse cultures.

One website designer I interviewed talked about the decision not to use *any* photos of people on the website, a decision he made in consultation with one of the pastors. This pastor and Web designer believe that photos of people are simply too proscriptive; they present too narrow a view of what the life of faith looks like. Neither do they use photos of the church building. Instead, they use photos that they believe are evocative of meaning, such as a bridge going off into the distance, symbolizing their congregation as a bridge between humans and God.

Another website producer talked about her desire to use photos that communicate that this congregation is a place of grace and redemption. Her congregation's website was noteworthy for the serene pictures of nature she had chosen in her effort to visually represent grace and redemption. In fact, many of the congregational websites in my study used photos of nature, which seemed to convey peace and serenity and could also indicate the congregation's concern for caring for creation.

The use of denominational graphics varies widely among congregations. In my research, most of the megachurches I studied were associated with a denomination. Yet very few of them used a graphic from the denomination on their home page, which seemed to communicate an attitude of autonomy on the part of these large churches. Their websites often convey that they are a community in themselves. Smaller churches associated with denominations were much more likely to use denominational graphics, which seemed to indicate their commitment to connections with other faith communities.

TELEPHONE BOOK LISTINGS

With more communication moving online, congregations may wonder whether it is worth paying for a listing or an advertisement in the yellow pages. The yellow pages can now be found online, so a listing often goes both in the paper and in the online versions, and it is a good idea to find out if this is the case.

Visitors staying in local hotels probably won't have Internet access but they will have a paper phone book in their room. I like to turn my computer off overnight, so if I need information about a church on Sunday morning, I am more likely to look at the paper yellow pages than the online version.

As a newcomer to a city, I can also attest to the frustration of a potential visitor when he or she finds that the telephone book listing for a congregation doesn't include the address of the congregation, something I have experienced more than once. Some congregations pay extra to get the worship service time listed in the telephone book, and I think that is a wise use of resources if the time of worship is stable.

Including Other Voices

When I began my study of congregational websites, I had no idea of the wide variety of things congregations are doing on their sites. Some congregations use their sites for activity sign-ups. Some enable online giving. Some have member-only pages, where members can log in and view directories of members, notes of board meetings, or enter into post-sermon discussions. Some have photo galleries where members can post photos from congregational activities. One website I viewed had more than eleven-thousand photos of a variety of congregational activities.

The possibility of responses by website visitors is a significant emerging issue. Website technology is becoming easier and less expensive to use, enabling a variety of responses. Some websites have online polls on the home page where website visitors can register their opinions about a topic. These polls generally have multiple-choice answers, so the range of answers is limited. Some congregations enable website visitors to send in open-ended answers to questions.

Other congregations are experimenting with online forums or groups where people can respond to each other. Blogs can also be structured so that readers can post comments automatically without any editing by the blog writer. This raises questions of appropriate content for congregational websites. Will people post comments that are destructive to the congregation or congregation members? How important is the free voicing of opinions on a congregational website? Do comments need to go through some sort of editing process before being posted? Congregational leaders need to make decisions about these issues.

Help from "Critical Friends"

When the Internet started to become a significant force in society about a decade ago, religious leaders were divided in their opinions about this new technology. Some were extremely negative, viewing the Internet as a dehumanizing force, a threat to community and communication. Others saw it as an opportunity for religious organizations, a place where proclamation and explanation could take place and community and connections could be nurtured.

One of the premier researchers on online religious community, Heidi Campbell, argues for a middle ground. She uses the term *critical friends* to describe what she would like to see: religious leaders who affirm the opportunities provided by the Internet, while also being cautious and careful about the possible negative repercussions.[1]

In my study of congregational websites, I found that this "critical friend" role was often absent in congregations. Many website producers work quite independently because of lack of interest or knowledge on the part of congregational leaders. Critical friends among the congregation's leaders would bring an additional set of eyes and an understanding of the congregation's priorities, enabling websites to represent congregations more accurately.

In addition, critical friends are urgently needed in congregations to minimize the growing tendency toward a consumerist model of faith and congregational life. Congregations are not commodities to be picked up and then discarded with every passing whim. Congregations demand commitment that is sometimes challenging and sometimes painful but also yields deep and meaningful fruit over time. Because websites use visual communication in similar ways to the advertising industry, congregational leaders need to think carefully about the ways their websites tap into consumerist practices.

The website producers I interviewed were uniformly positive about the opportunity afforded by the medium. Most of them saw no potential conflicts in wholesale adoption of secular marketing strategies to promote their congregation and to describe its uniqueness. Critical friends, with an awareness of the risks inherent in the consumer model and perhaps with theological training, need to be in dialogue with website producers as choices are made regarding website content.

Careful and effective use of congregational websites will involve attention to the visual as well as the verbal and will reflect the congregation's values in photos, graphics, art, and links. Website producers will not work in isolation but with the help of critical friends among the congregation's leaders who will help them make decisions about this powerful communication tool.

Websites provide opportunities for congregations to reach out to potential visitors and provide information and resources for members. Along with welcome brochures printed on paper, websites offer congregations a platform for expressing what is important to them and who they are. They are a place for strategic self-presentation that will likely become even more important in years to come.

TELEPHONE ANSWERING SYSTEMS

The audience for the congregational answering systems is the same as the audience for websites: members and visitors. Members need to be able to get information about programs and leave messages for staff. Separate mailboxes for pastoral staff are very helpful so that members can leave private messages for specific individuals.

Visitors need to be able to access basic information about the congregation, including the address, time of worship services, and website address. This basic information for visitors can be in the main message, or if the congregation has a more complex system, the basic information can be on a secondary message.

I have listened to many answering machine messages that don't include the time of worship. Because I recently moved to a new city and visited numerous churches, I can attest to the level of frustration that visitors feel when they call the church on a Saturday night or Sunday morning hoping to get the time of the worship service off the answering machine and it's not there.

The Internet is becoming increasingly significant as a means of communication, particularly among younger generations. As of late 2007, more than 70 percent of the people in North America used the Internet. One study showed a significant shift that happened in 2007: sixteen- to twenty-four-year-olds now spend more time online than watching television.

A recent experience highlights this shift. A friend's son, twenty-four, was traveling in our area with one of his friends, and my husband and I hosted them for several days. They were interested in visiting one of the nature centers in our area, so we showed them guidebooks with descriptions of the centers, gave them phone numbers to call for information, and handed them the cordless phone. They set the phone aside, glanced briefly at the descriptions in the guidebooks, and immediately pulled out their laptops to visit the websites of the nature centers in order to make the decision about which one to visit.

If congregations are serious about welcoming younger generations into their communities of faith, they need to pay careful attention to their presence on the Internet. With the yellow pages increasingly moving online, it makes sense to have a well-thought-out online presence. And if congregational leaders are serious about wise use of resources, they can't ignore the many ways a well-designed website can serve a congregation and help shape its future.

Questions for Reflection, Journaling, and Discussion

1. Who develops and maintains your congregation's website? What are the advantages and disadvantages of the way you currently do it? Are there people in your congregation who function as critical friends of the website?
2. Does the visual communication on your congregation's website mesh with the verbal communication? Do both accurately represent the values of the congregation?
3. Look at your congregation's website through the eyes of a newcomer to see if all your immediate questions would be answered. Look at your website through the eyes of a member seeking sermon downloads or information about events.
4. How "slick" and professional do you want your website to be? Do you want to modify secular advertising and marketing techniques in some way to reflect your values?

5 | Communicating Right Now

Blogs and E-mail

IN ADDITION TO CONGREGATIONAL WEBSITES, blogs and e-mail are two more faces of the Internet that have significance for congregations. Blogs are much newer than e-mail and the part they play in congregational life will probably increase. E-mail has been around longer and appears to be here to stay, a daily reality for most congregations.

Both blogs and e-mail are forms of immediate communication for virtually no cost. As recently as several decades ago, this combination of immediacy and frugality was unimaginable in written communication. A congregational website is usually constructed carefully, often with a team of people making suggestions and contributing content. But blogs and e-mail can be instantaneous. I can fire off an e-mail that will be received within seconds, and I can create a blog post that can be viewed almost immediately.

In this chapter we will consider issues raised by blogs and e-mail that need to be considered by congregational leaders, particularly the connection between communication of the congregation's values and identity and these two communication tools.

What Are Blogs?

Blogs—originally called Web logs—created by pastors, rabbis, and other religious leaders, as well as by congregation members, are becoming more common. Blogs are a type of website with one major identifying characteristic. The entries on a blog are dated, and the most recent entries appear first. A blog usually contains verbal text, and it can also include photos, video, and links to other websites. The word *blog* can be used a noun, describing the particular kind of website, and the word can also be used as a verb, the action of assembling materials for a blog and posting them online.

Blogs are more like diaries than any other form of website is, and it is no accident that the country with the most blogs, Japan, has a long history of diary writing.[1]

A blog can be used like a diary for recording responses to specific events or issues on particular dates. A blog can also be more like a weekly or monthly newsletter column, carefully crafted like a newsletter article would be. Both of these styles of blog entries are commonly used by ministers and rabbis.

Blogs are easy to set up using common blog websites like WordPress and Blogger, which are free and have many attractive templates for users. Because they are inexpensive and easy to use, blogs offer a lot of communication impact for a small cost in time and money.

Why Blog?

The opportunities offered by blogs for people in congregational leadership are manifold. First, they provide one more way for congregational leaders to communicate in a personal and authentic style about things that matter. Because the diary medium stands behind blogs, communication on blogs is expected to reflect honest emotions and personal experiences. Some degree of intimacy is a characteristic of communication on blogs, something that is exactly right for our time with the growing emphasis on authenticity and personal connections that is apparent in so many forms of new media.

Blogs are a perfect medium to tell stories about what faith looks like in practice. Testimonies, stories about people whose lives are being changed because of their faith, and stories about those who are serving in the community or overseas are perfect for blogs.

Because blog entries are always connected to specific dates, blogs provide the opportunity to discuss current events in the wider culture and their connection to faith. Upcoming congregational events and ministries can be described in order to encourage people to participate. Toward the end of each week, aspects of the upcoming worship service can be highlighted, with an encouragement to invite neighbors and friends. Recent events can be described as a way to talk about the significance of what happened or the way God was present in those events.

Brian Bailey and Terry Storch, authors of *The Blogging Church*, talk about blogs as the perfect place to share "the why behind the what."[2] The worship folder and the congregation's website might give the date and time of the kickoff event for a new ministry, perhaps a new children's program, an outreach into the community, or an upcoming mission trip. The minister's blog or the congregation's blog are good places to explain why the ministry is starting, what motivated its leaders to dream it up, and what they hope participants will gain from it.

A blog entry can convey "the why behind the what" by telling the personal hopes of the leaders. Or the blog can tell a story that lies behind the dream. A blog post could give a personal testimony about a similar ministry in another congregation or from last year's version of the same ministry. The vision for the ministry can be addressed in a personal and honest way.

Who are we as a congregation and what matters to us? What do we care about and why? Stories and descriptions of upcoming and past events told in the light of these central questions are perfect for blogs.

The Narrative Structure of Blogs

Blogs offer a place for a communication style that is growing more common in the twenty-first century. In our time, truths are seldom laid out in a systematic, linear fashion, in long mission statements with numerous points, or in long documents with complicated arguments. Instead, meaning is communicated in stories and metaphors, through photos, and through brief teaching statements. Even blogs that feature essay-style articles will generally use shorter entries than a paper magazine or newsletter.

A congregation's blog entries can be viewed as a series of building blocks, each one communicating a piece of what the congregation considers to be valuable and essential for faith. In many ways, this lightens the pressure on the person writing the blog entry. Each blog post needs to tell only a part of the whole story, to vividly and faithfully represent something about this congregation's identity and values, but it doesn't have to say everything. An ideal blog post is only two- to three-hundred words, which is only a few paragraphs. It can make only one point or tell one brief story.

And a blog post is conversational and casual. A man who blogs regularly told me he pounds out his blog posts with very little revision, which he believes makes them more like talking than like traditional writing. He considers himself not to be expounding on an idea or expressing his opinion as much as he is initiating a conversation.

A blog post is like a short sermon in that it can really only make one point. One of the major challenges for new preachers is to realize that each sermon needs to have one central focus and develop one main idea. No one sermon can say everything about the life of faith. A person who preaches regularly hopes and prays that, over time, all those sermons will serve as building blocks to communicate the big picture of God's goodness and the faith journey God invites us into.

In the same way, blog posts don't have to say everything about the congregation, just one thing told in a compelling way, one piece of the big picture of the congregation's life. In that way, blogs are different from congregational websites, which need to represent in a more systematic way the life of the congregation.

Blog posts accumulate over time. Viewers can scroll backwards to see the development of thoughts over months and even years. The building blocks that are created with each blog post remain online for people to access if they want to. Therefore, some consistency in the values expressed is a good idea.

Because blogs are free, with their only cost being the labor to produce them, some congregations are using blogs as their main website. I want to discourage this practice. Blogs and websites are both helpful, but in different ways. Congregational websites require an investment of time and money that is well worth making. A congregational website can give an overview of a congregation and its values and identity at one glance much more effectively than a blog. Using a more personal style, a blog presents those values and identity in pieces that build on each other over time.

Building Trust on Blogs

One of the challenges of blog writing is to build the kind of trust among readers that will keep them coming back to the blog. Blog readers come to depend on a certain frequency of posts; therefore, developing a fairly consistent pattern for timing new blog posts plays a role in attracting readers. People stop looking at blogs if nothing new is posted.

Links are an integral part of all websites, including blogs. Links serve readers by pointing them to other websites or blogs that you have found interesting or helpful. "Here's a blog post I really liked about children's ministries." "Here's a link to a website with resources about spiritual gifts." When readers visit the sites you have linked to and find them helpful, they grow in trusting you as a resource.

In the same way, quotations from other websites or from books help build trust on blogs because they allow the reader to see you as a source of interesting information. (Be sure to give credit for quotations and others' ideas.)

Lists are increasingly popular on personal websites like Facebook and MySpace. Using lists on blog posts can effectively engage readers. Topics on a congregational blog might include the following:

- Top five sermon downloads this year from our website
- Most popular books checked out of the congregation's library
- Upcoming sermon scriptures
- Number of kids in the various religious education classes
- Favorite movies, books, or blogs of the congregation's staff or board members

Lists on a minister's blog might include favorite books, movies, songs, or hobbies; insights from a recent conference; or Scripture passages on a specific topic.

The way a blog ends its life also contributes to maintaining trust. When a blog has outlived its usefulness or when the people writing for it have simply run out of steam or moved onto new projects, the best strategy is to post an entry saying that this blog is no longer being updated. It is also an opportunity for the blog writers to mention their newest projects and perhaps give the address of a new blog. A deliberate end communicates that the blogger cares about the readers.

Writing for the Congregation's Blog

Many blogs related to congregations are the solo product of the minister, who uses the blog to talk about the congregation's life, reflect on current events, and describe his or her faith journey. Coming up with a blog post every week, or several times a week, can be quite a challenge for one person.

To relieve some of the pressure on ministers and pastors, congregations should consider the possibility of a congregational blog, a joint production of a team of people. Someone needs to be responsible for overseeing the blog, but several people can do the writing. Perhaps the senior minister writes a few posts each month, while others—associate ministers, congregational lay leaders, other staff—are also responsible for one or two posts every month. Posts can be brief: a story, a quotation from a book, a short reflection on a Scripture passage, a description of an upcoming event and why it was planned.

Members of the blog team need to enjoy and appreciate the blogging medium. Effective blog posts cannot simply be recycled announcements from the bulletin, newsletters, or website. They cannot be official pronouncements or minutes from meetings. Because honesty, authenticity, and a personal approach are essential on a blog, team members need to understand the significance of these characteristics in communicating the congregation's identity and values.

Bailey and Storch, in *The Blogging Church*, suggest that individual ministries within a congregation can set up their own blogs so that new volunteers can get up to speed quickly on the ministry, potential recruits can get an idea of what they might do, and volunteers can stay informed about the planning for upcoming events.

They cite the example of a blog for children's ministry volunteers and they give an example of ten things that could be posted on the blog:

- A welcome statement for new volunteers, with photos and an introduction
- A description of an upcoming event, the vision that lies behind the event, and the need for volunteers
- A spotlight on a volunteer
- Celebration of birthdays and milestones
- Prayer requests
- The week's lesson with a link that enables volunteers to download it
- Stories about what's happening in the ministry
- Answers to commonly asked questions
- Photos from recent events

- Introductions of the children's ministries staff, done in a fun way[3]

In the same way that a the person in charge of a congregation's blog can ask a group of people to contribute to the blog, the blog of ministry area can have numerous contributors who submit photos, write short descriptions of events, and tell stories. However, someone needs to have ownership and oversight of the blog to keep its vision and coherence strong.

Starting to Blog

A blog can be one more forum for conveying a congregation's heart and soul, what its leaders care about and why. For that reason, the value of having a blog is worth considering. In addition, the very existence of a blog connected to a congregation communicates a set of values, such as the importance of informal and personal communication and a desire for feedback and conversation among a congregation's members and visitors.

Before you create your own blog, be sure that you have read a good number blogs over several weeks, at least. Observe the kind of material people post on blogs and pay attention to the kind of language typically used on blogs.

In addition, a few specific questions must be addressed and the answers must be clear in your mind. If you are in a leadership role in a congregation, the first question that must be addressed is whether the blog is yours or the congregation's. Bailey and Storch suggest that one way to get at that question is to think about what would happen if you left that congregation. Would you continue to write on that same blog, or would you leave it behind for another leader in that congregation to continue? The answer to this question will affect the next set of questions that need to be answered.

Is the blog personal, professional, or organizational? The best professional and organizational blogs have a personal voice, so

BLOGS: A CAUTIONARY TALE

A man I will call James is the minister of a thriving urban church. James has a well-known and widely read blog, characterized by his lack of fear in taking on challenging topics and putting forth controversial opinions. In part because of his blog, he was asked to write a column in his local newspaper. In the column, he continued his practice of writing bluntly about topics related to faith.

James's columns drew a lot of letters to the editor because of the controversial positions he advocated. However, it wasn't a newspaper column that led to his removal as a columnist. It was a blog entry in which he expressed an opinion that went too far over the line for many readers. That blog entry precipitated an avalanche of letters to the newspaper demanding he be stripped of his monthly column.

Should ministers avoid controversial topics on blogs? Should they be careful not to offend anyone? How controversial is too controversial? Because blogs draw on the diary medium, they need to have some degree of informality and intimacy, opening up conversation and interaction. However, bloggers need to be careful not to be sloppy or careless in the opinions they express. Bloggers need to remember that their posts can be read very widely by serious, critical readers. Blogs are public documents that can be cited and circulated far beyond a congregation.

these three categories have a lot of overlap, but there is still a distinction that should be explored before beginning a blog.

A personal blog is for friends and family. A minister or rabbi in a congregation needs to be careful in creating a personal blog, because in those roles one's personal life and professional life overlap greatly, and if a blog can be accessed by anyone, then unexpected readers will almost certainly find the blog.

A professional blog for a person in ministry centers on that ministry, what you are thinking, feeling, and wondering about your ministry. A professional blog by a minister or rabbi can be widely advertised, including a link from the congregation's website.

An organizational blog centers on the congregation and is usually written by a few people rather than just one person. It should be integrally related to the congregation's website.

One additional question should be addressed before starting a blog: Who is the blog for? Congregation members, staff members, volunteers, or leaders? People who have never attended church? Teenagers? University students? The voice you use on the blog will vary slightly from one audience to the next.

Because unexpected readers are almost always a part of blogging, anyone creating a blog can be fairly sure that some people who are not in the intended audience will read the blog. A good idea before posting is to read over each blog entry as if through the eyes of unexpected readers.

However, keeping a fresh and authentic voice is also important. In an effort not to offend anyone, the voice on a blog can become bland and flavorless. Writing with passion and a personal approach is essential for a blog to work. Admitting mistakes and being willing to face criticism contribute to the authenticity that makes blogging so effective in our time.

Building Community through Blogs

Blogs can be set up to allow reader responses or not, and that presents one of the ongoing challenges for congregations of the new electronic media. If a blog is identified with a congregation, then what happens if someone responds to a blog entry in a way that is inappropriate?

One obvious solution is to set up the congregation's blog in such a way that responses are not permitted. The blog then becomes one more form of one-way communication. Most people who visit blogs are there to read, not comment, so this option is not a bad way to begin a congregational blog.

Another solution is to take a risk and see what happens. People who read a lot of blogs are used to seeing places for responses, and most responses are brief and appropriate. And in any case, many blog posts simply don't get comments. Leaving the option for comments expresses a willingness to hear congregation members' voices, so why not allow the option for comments, to reflect the congregation's value that all voices are welcome? This option allows for comments but doesn't really hope for them, expect them, or get too excited about them.

A third way of looking at a congregation's blog is to welcome and invite comments, to expect the blog to grow into a genuine forum for online community. This option flows out of a more decentralized view of congregational communication that welcomes a diversity of voices as an authentic expression of Christian community. Readers of the blog can be invited to post the addresses of their own blogs along with their comments.

Some congregations require a log-in process in order to post comments on a blog. This eliminates the possibility that random visitors to the blog will post their thoughts. This strategy might help congregations feel safer as they begin to blog, with less fear that inappropriate comments will be posted.

Currently many ministers have their own blogs, but not many congregations have blogs that are created by a team of people to reflect the life of the congregation. So the challenges inherent in encouraging comments on a congregational blog have not yet been explored. But because the blogging medium most often allows and welcomes comments, my best guess is that blogging for congregations will be a way to encourage interaction and conversation.

Blogs have a distinctive voice: conversational, personal, and informal. They speak the language of our culture and time. Congregations and congregational leaders can use blogs wisely and strategically to communicate the heart and soul of a congregation. This medium has great communication potential for communities of faith.

Next I want to turn to an older form of Internet communication: e-mail. It has in common with blogging the characteristics of immediacy and informality, which seem to be typical of communication in the twenty-first century. E-mail appears to be here to stay as a significant form of communication used by congregations. Values and identity need to be considered in an approach to e-mail.

The Challenge of E-mail

Ask almost anyone over forty about the way e-mail has changed his or her working life, and you will get an earful. Some people love e-mail, some hate it, but almost no one says that work is the same as it was fifteen or twenty years ago. E-mail has changed working life in almost every setting, including congregations.

When I served as an associate pastor, I heard a lot of complaints from other people in ministry about the time it takes to deal with e-mail each day. So I decided to convene an "e-mail lunch" for the pastoral staff at my own church and some neighboring congregations. (It goes without saying that I sent out an e-mail invitation to the lunch!) We ate our sack lunches and talked about the gifts and weaknesses of e-mail, the ironies and pastoral concerns we have noticed.

The comments people made at that lunch several years ago are still relevant and helpful today. We agreed that e-mail is a gift in certain situations. E-mail is great for the following purposes:

- Reminders
- Getting out information regarding meetings, times, details
- Quick compliments
- Brief questions
- Some kinds of scheduling

In some cases, e-mail can be helpful in clarifying thoughts. A youth pastor told the story of a convoluted conflict he had with a volunteer. The two of them talked for a long time and made no headway. Finally the youth pastor said, "Why don't you write down the issues you're concerned about in an e-mail?" The writing process evidently helped the volunteer think more clearly, and, after the e-mail, the two of them were able to settle their conflict. Some people definitely process ideas better in writing than verbally, and e-mail can make that possible in an informal way.

However, other people are much clearer with the spoken word than with writing. Another pastor told about a very painful e-mail he received from an elder. Following up with a phone call, he tried to clarify the issues raised in the e-mail by summarizing what he thought the elder was saying. The elder kept responding, "Oh, I didn't mean that at all. . . . What I really meant was this. . . ." The e-mail had come across as harsh and accusatory, and the elder evidently didn't feel that way at all.

A related concern about e-mail is that electronic communication can happen without sufficient thought or prayer. Difficult questions can be answered in a rapid-fire, cavalier way, and the answer can seem superficial or insensitive. E-mail seems to encourage a stream of consciousness style that can lack both civility and careful thought. E-mail also makes it harder to check in with the person on the other end. It is harder to say, "What did you mean when you just said that?"

Everyone agreed that e-mail is not appropriate for confrontations or negative feedback. Having received a few e-mail "blast-o-grams" myself, I heartily agree. If a comment is positive or encouraging, e-mail can get that feedback to people quickly. But if something is negative or sensitive, usually it should be said in person or discussed in a phone call so that tone of voice can be factored into the discussion and clarifying questions can be asked immediately.

The people who attended my e-mail lunch were all decisive and clear about the dangers of confrontation and conflict by e-mail. In the years since that lunch, as e-mail has become even more common in workplace and ministry situations, I have become more convinced they were absolutely right. It is simply too easy to whip out an e-mail expressing critical thoughts. If there is one

---

GUIDELINES FOR TEXTING

Sending text messages using a cell phone is an increasingly significant part of youth ministry. One particular youth minister sends three texts each week to every student in her youth group. Some of those texts are sent to the whole group, but some of them are individual words of encouragement and follow-up on face-to-face conversations.

Many of the same guidelines for e-mails apply to text messages. Texting is great for reminders, brief and basic information, and for compliments. But texting is not appropriate for sending criticism, no matter how constructive it is. A discussion among congregational leaders and staff about appropriate and wise use of text messages will be profitable and helpful.

---

e-mail guideline that congregations should always establish, it is that difficult conversations should always be conducted in person or over the phone rather than by e-mail. This policy reflects a congregation's commitment to healthy resolution of conflict.

At the e-mail lunch, some pastors expressed concern that relying on e-mail will enable people to avoid relationships. I noted that the reverse can also be true. I told about the time that a man in our congregation lost his mother. Several others on our pastoral staff were closer to that man than I was, and they had asked him verbally how he was coping. They got little response. I had to e-mail him about a scheduling detail, and in the e-mail I asked him about his mourning. He answered me at length, expressing in his e-mail reply his feelings of sadness and loss, the first such expression to anyone on our staff. I viewed this as a healthy form of grief, appropriate for a very reserved person. Others wondered if he needed to be encouraged to share with someone face-to-face about what he was feeling.

Length, Permanence, and Timing of E-mails

Several pastors said they never write long e-mails. One pastor has a two-paragraph rule. If it takes longer than two paragraphs to write, it needs to happen in a conversation. These pastors reply by saying things like, "Call my secretary and schedule a phone conversation with me." Or, "Those are good issues. Let's talk about them at the next committee meeting." Or, "I definitely want to talk with you about what you have written. Can you grab me after church this Sunday and we'll spend a few minutes together?"

Writing short e-mails saves time, and it can help prevent a newly emerging nightmare in ministry. Anything we write can be forwarded on. When we don't want certain thoughts on a sensitive topic to circulate, we have to be vigilant not to give in to the temptation just to say a few things in an e-mail. E-mail feels less permanent than a paper letter. That's why a compliment written with a pen on a card can feel more significant than an e-mail compliment. However, e-mail does have a potential permanence that we can't ignore.

A related issue is the fact that most e-mail programs automatically keep the previous e-mails on the same topic. Sometimes after a long exchange by two people, an e-mail gets forwarded to someone else or a group of people. Sometimes those people need to see the whole discussion, but sometimes the whole discussion has aspects that are private and personal. Be very careful when forwarding e-mail that comes at the end of a long discussion. Church secretaries and administrators, who may be responsible for forwarding e-mails from pastors, ministers, and rabbis, need to be alerted to this challenge.

Another challenge relates to the timing of replies to e-mail. A growing number of people in our congregations work in offices where they are expected to keep their e-mail turned on all day, answering questions as they come. These folks may expect their minister or rabbi to do the same thing. One pastor uses an automatic reply to all her e-mails, saying she answers e-mail once a day and saying which day she takes off each week.

Ministers and rabbis may be tempted to leave their e-mail on all day, allowing each new message to pop up on the screen. Several pastors said that one of their greatest disciplines is to turn their e-mail off and put limits around the time they are willing to spend each day with e-mail. Everyone with whom I talked said that without limits, e-mail can consume an ever-growing share of their time. "I have to turn it off and simply not notice if I have new messages," one pastor said. "Otherwise I get sucked in. And besides, no one needs an answer that fast."

Some pastors have found they need to discipline themselves not to read their e-mail first thing in the morning. They need to save their best energy for the most important aspects of their ministry and save e-mail for a time of day when energy is lower.

E-mail Guidelines for Congregational Leaders

In many congregations, a discussion among leaders—paid and unpaid, ordained and lay—about appropriate use of e-mail would bear good fruit. Many of the issues raised in the e-mail lunch I hosted could be discussed. A conscious e-mail strategy for congregational leaders can reflect the values of the community.

E-mail can be encouraged for positive feedback, brief questions, scheduling, and disseminating information. It should be discouraged in conflict situations because tone of voice and the ability to ask questions are so necessary for managing challenging issues. E-mail should also be discouraged for sensitive issues so that confidentiality is respected.

All of these strategies and actions relate to congregational values in the area of nurturing good relationships. These actions speak. They say that compliments matter, that the congregation is a community of people who encourage each other. They say that up-to-date scheduling information matters, that leaders want to honor people's time and schedules. They say that conflict mat-

WATCH OUT FOR FATIGUE

Sending e-mails and text messages is, in some ways, too easy. It is simply too easy to send a thoughtless reply, to answer a complex question before thinking about the best way to respond, or to sound critical when that was not what we intended.

The risk of sending a potentially damaging reply is magnified by fatigue. I have found that after a certain time in the evening, I should limit myself to reading e-mails without replying. I need to avoid the temptation to answer just a few e-mails late at night because my answers are simply not well thought-out. I can read the e-mails at night, and then let the questions and issues raised by the e-mails percolate overnight in my thoughts. My answers the next day will be much more coherent and much less likely to get me into trouble of some sort.

ters, that the congregation is committed to dealing with conflict carefully and intentionally in a personal way. Ultimately, these actions say that a congregation values good relationships in the community of faith so highly that leaders are willing to take the time to consider the ways technology can be used to nurture relationships. They want to avoid the pitfalls that can come from careless use of technology.

Part of a discussion about e-mail guidelines should include the question of whether committees and task forces can conduct their business by e-mail rather than face-to-face meetings. In my years as an associate pastor, I served on a minor committee that almost never met in person. We conducted all our infrequent business by e-mail, and everyone on the committee was content to have it that way. We saw one another in other settings, so we remained relationally connected.

If committees and task forces are going to function by e-mail, the question of relational connections between the people must be considered. Over time, if all business is conducted by e-mail and the people don't nurture personal connections, conflict can arise simply because the people don't know each other. A guideline could be established for committees that meet by e-mail, suggesting that they meet in person at least once a year for sharing, prayer, and a chance to get to know each other beyond the confines of the business they transact by e-mail the rest of the year.

The timing of replies to e-mail is another area where congregational values are expressed in actions. Usually an e-mail address is posted prominently on the congregation's website so that website visitors can ask questions. How soon will those e-mails be answered? Expecting instant answers may put too much pressure on congregational staff, but long-delayed answers communicate something negative about the congregation's care for members and outsiders. Something in the middle should be articulated.

The timing of replies by congregational staff and lay leaders to e-mails from members also needs to be discussed and articulated. How soon is soon enough? How long is too long? Do instant replies communicate that the congregation has bought into the culture's values, or do rapid replies communicate love and caring? These are not questions that should occupy hours of discussion, but they should be considered with some degree of care because actions play a part in communicating values.

Connections between people matter. I cannot imagine a community of faith that would disagree with that statement. Because e-mail facilitates connections in significant ways in our time, its use in congregations is worthy of reflection.

Replacing Paper Communication

At that e-mail lunch several years ago, several people mentioned that e-mail can replace some communication on paper, saving money and trees. Increasingly in congregations, reports from committees and leadership boards are circulated by e-mail. Announcements regarding upcoming events increasingly appear by e-mail.

More congregations are using weekly or monthly e-mails in place of printed newsletters. The newsletters often include photos or graphics, a letter from the minister, worship schedules, Scripture readings, announcements about events, and prayer requests. They may include links to denominational or mission agencies, to the congregation's website, or to a blog associated with the congregation.

A weekly e-mail or monthly e-mail newsletter can consolidate numerous random e-mails. Someone recently told me about the barrage of e-mails she gets from her diocese, and I encouraged her to suggest that the diocese establish a weekly or monthly e-mail newsletter so that priests and lay leaders can get all the information in a consistent, coherent package rather than randomly. In addition, sending out information in an e-mail newsletter format rather than a series of separate e-mails encourages concise announcements rather than long, rambling epistles.

In most congregations, not everyone uses e-mail, so a means to get the same information to people who are not online must be considered. In one congregation that sends a weekly e-mail, that e-mail is printed out and several copies are made. Those copies are placed in the sanctuary for people to pick up. The people who pick up the paper version of the e-mail don't have the advantage of getting the Scripture readings in advance of the worship service, but they do get the message from the minister, the prayer requests, and the announcements.

Printing a few copies says that everyone in the congregation matters. Sending a weekly or monthly e-mail says that financial and environmental stewardship matter. These are congregational values that are communicated through actions related to e-mail.

Another way to honor congregation members with differing computer skills and different computers and levels of online connection is to check with a variety of congregation members regarding their reception of the online newsletter. Does it download fairly quickly? Do they have any problems reading it? Perhaps fewer photos and graphics would make the newsletter quicker to download. Perhaps different fonts would make it easier to read. Just because an e-mail works well on one computer doesn't mean it will work well on another.

Blogs and E-mail

Twenty or thirty years ago, who could have imagined the kind of instant communication now available through blogs and e-mail? I live several thousand miles from most of my family members, but I can communicate with them instantly through e-mail. I can post a photo on my blog and they can see it right away.

I have lived overseas before, and I remember the time lag between writing letters and waiting for a reply. I can remember taking photos on film, getting them printed, and then mailing them to family members to give them idea of my life in another place. All of that has changed.

I can also remember the challenge in congregational life of arranging meeting times by phone and trying to disseminate information about a change of venue by word of mouth. I can remember when sermons and newsletters were the only places to discuss the vision that lay behind an upcoming event. All that has changed because of e-mail, websites, and blogs.

People joke about how ridiculous it is to send e-mails to people working just down the hall, and surely these new media do manifest some strange and illogical excesses. But they are changing or have already changed the way much communication happens. Some of the changes are healthy and helpful and some are ineffective and downright silly. Congregational leaders need to discuss the ways and places these new communication technologies intersect with the heart-and-soul values of the congregation.

Questions for Reflection, Journaling, and Discussion

1. Have you read any blogs you like? What did you like about them? Have you seen blogs tell stories effectively? What made the storytelling work well?
2. In what ways might a blog make sense for your congregation or for a ministry within your congregation? What could a blog accomplish that would help you meet your goals?
3. What do you like and dislike about e-mail? What guidelines for e-mail use have you developed, either consciously or unconsciously? In what ways do those values reflect values you consider to be important?
4. Does your congregation have stated or unstated guidelines for e-mail use? If you were to list a few e-mail guidelines you would like to see your congregational leaders adopt, what would they be?
5. Are text messages used in any of the ministries in your congregation? Have any discussions focused on wise use of text messages?

6 | Online Community

IN THE EARLY AND MID-1990s, WHEN ONLINE bulletin boards and Internet groups were in their infancy, some religious leaders sounded an alarm about online community. Online relationships couldn't possibly be "real" community, they argued, and online opportunities for religious connection would seriously undercut congregational life. They believed that relationships in a technological environment would be arid, sterile, and soulless, and they encouraged religious leaders to approach online connections very cautiously.

In contrast, some people in high tech communities argued that here, at last, was the opportunity for truly democratic communication. When people meet online, they said, everyone would be equal. Gender, social status, and educational background would be eliminated as significant factors, and all voices would be respected and valued equally. The result would be a new kind community based purely on people's ideas rather than economic or educational status, a place for utopian communication and democracy.

More than a decade later, we have seen that both of these views turned out to be too simplistic. While many religious leaders are still cautious about the online relationships, actual experience has demonstrated that many people have nurtured significant connections online. And while political blogs have brought about a kind of journalistic democracy previously unseen, the hopes for true egalitarian democracy online have faded. Experience has shown

us that status exists in online communication like it exists everywhere else. Markers of Internet status have emerged, including
indicators such as writing skills, familiarity with online jargon,
and abilities to create links to blogs and YouTube clips.

The online environment offers congregations many opportunities for connection. Cautious and careful embrace of these
opportunities involves considering numerous issues. I will begin
by telling a few stories related to online community.

What's Missing in My Congregation

Steve is the pastor of a small congregation in a small city. A few
years ago, Steve contracted kidney disease and ended up on dialysis, waiting for a kidney transplant. The members of his congregation were supportive and showered Steve and his wife and family
with love. But something was missing. They longed for contact
with others who had experienced the ordeal of dialysis, particularly other Christians who had remained faithful to God and who
had experienced God's presence and love in the midst of it.

A friend of Steve's participated in an online group for people
who had lost a family member, and he encouraged Steve to look
online for support. Steve found a few online support groups for
people with kidney disease, but none of them had a Christian
focus. Still, he enjoyed reading the comments of people who had
experienced the same disease.

Steve decided to start an online group for Christians with
kidney disease. He signed up with Yahoo to create a group, and
over the next year about thirty people joined his group. A couple of
years later, the group was still going strong. Membership doubled,
then tripled. Still only about twenty to thirty people posted comments regularly, but the identity of those twenty to thirty people
changed over time. Some people seemed to stop needing such
intense support, and new people joined in.

An online group usually enables people to post comments
and questions that other group members may read and respond

to when they sign on to the group. Group members can sign up to receive daily e-mails summarizing the posts. They can also choose to get an e-mail every time someone posts a message, or they can choose not to receive e-mails and simply go to the group website to view the messages group members have posted. In some groups, old posts are archived indefinitely so that members can search through old posts to find topics they want to read about. All of these options were available for the members of Steve's group.

A couple years after his transplant, Steve no longer needed the group with the same intensity, but he could see that the group was fulfilling a significant need. So he continued to function as the moderator.

In his role as moderator, Steve reads the posts. He occasionally deletes posts because they are rude and inappropriate. A few times he has denied people access to the group because of their consistent rudeness. But by and large he sees people listening, caring, and expressing a commitment to pray for each other as they work through pain and look for God's presence in their challenges.

Steve is convinced that online groups can provide significant support that supplements congregational life. Perhaps in large cities it is possible for people of faith to find face-to-face support groups that address their specific situation, but even in large cities most people would have to leave their own congregation to find such groups. He sees clearly that in smaller towns and rural areas there simply aren't enough people who have experienced the same specific situations to provide support for each other.

Online community offers another significant advantage in the midst of a fast-paced life. Whenever Steve was feeling sad about his health challenges, he could log on to the group, even if it was the middle of the night. He didn't have to make room in his schedule for a support group on a certain night of the week at a certain time.

His involvement in the online group didn't negate the loving care of the people in his congregation. It didn't make him feel that his congregation was incomplete or without value. The group simply met a need that his congregation couldn't fill.

Other Kinds of Groups

I recently joined a Yahoo group for church administrators so that I could search their archives for information about church websites. The group receives one or two dozen posts each day related to payroll, benefits, building use, weddings, and other administrative issues. People in administrative jobs in churches ask questions and get answers to their questions. Because of the specialized nature of their jobs, they receive support from each other in a way they can't get from other people in their congregation.

The last time I counted, Yahoo had more than 150,000 groups. And that's only Yahoo. Google and other websites provide places for groups. The topics relate to every subject under the sun.

A list serve is another kind of online group, a group of people who can easily send e-mails to everyone in the group. Sandra is the minister of a congregation that uses the lectionary for focusing weekly worship on the seasons and festivals of church year. Sandra belongs to a list serve of other ministers who discuss the lectionary readings in preparation for preaching.

In Sandra's list serve, the participants send e-mails about the passages in the lectionary. They write down significant insights about the passages and pose questions about the passages. Some of the members then post the sermon they have come up with from the passages.

Sandra describes herself as a "lurker." In an online community, those who read the content but don't make comments are called lurkers. Most of the people in Sandra's list serve are lurkers; fewer than half of the members post comments.

When I was a PhD student, all the graduate students in my department participated in a list serve. I got several e-mails every day from list-serve members. Participants asked questions about footnote software and other computer programs, inquired about courses and professors, traded resources for research, and congratulated each other when important academic milestones were passed. I mostly lurked on that group for three years, learning all kinds of things about graduate study, until it came time to sell my car. I got a buyer from among the other graduate students by sending out a notice on the list serve.

A list serve is a formal e-mail group, set up using mailing list software. Many people participate in informal e-mail groups simply by creating a group list in their own e-mail software. Within congregations, people send e-mails to others in various informal e-mail groups. This includes members of committees, staff of congregations, members of Bible study groups, and participants in midweek worship services or other special worship events. A list serve becomes helpful when the group grows so large that keeping track of members' e-mail address changes is difficult.

The relationships formed in Yahoo and Google groups generally begin online, and sometimes move to face-to-face relationships when the people realize they would like to meet those with whom they talk online. Some relationships move in the opposite direction. They begin face-to-face and then develop an online component as well. I was in a prayer support group for many years. We met monthly to share prayer requests and pray for each other. Early in our years together, I might talk on the phone with one or two of the group members between meetings, but we often went a whole month without contact with each other.

As e-mail became more common, and as each of us checked our e-mail more often, we got in the habit of writing e-mails to the group between meetings. We reported answers to prayer, and we asked for prayer for needs that had emerged since the last meeting. Although I have moved away from the group members, we still have active e-mail contact with each other. The rest of them meet together monthly to share and pray together, but I still feel included and supported from many miles away.

That prayer group uses e-mail to supplement its face-to-face meetings, which is becoming more common in a number of settings as e-mail has become a familiar way of communicating. But in my case, the online component of the group is my main connection.

WHY LIST SERVES?

My recent experience with a midweek worship service group illustrates why list serves are helpful for larger groups. (The word is sometimes spelled "listserv," which actually refers to an early list serve software.) A church in my city has a small midweek service, and a group of us get together for dinner before the service. Whoever feels motivated to host the dinner sends an e-mail telling everyone they are willing to host.

When I joined the dinner group, one man was acting as the coordinator of the dinner, and he kept an updated e-mail list of the two to three dozen people who had expressed interest. If someone was willing to host, that potential host sent an e-mail to the man with the updated e-mail list, and he then sent an e-mail to the whole group. He moved away several months ago, and the group continues to gather for dinner, but no one keeps track of the updated list of members. So when people send out an e-mail saying they are willing to host the dinner, they just hit "Reply All" on the e-mail about the previous dinner.

A new fellow has been coming to the group, and one person in the group always forwards the e-mail to him. And another person changed her e-mail address. Getting these changes into the e-mail group list is a bit confusing because now no one keeps the updated list. A list serve would require someone to be in charge of the e-mail list, but it would provide a simple structure to keep e-mail addresses updated for the group. Each week the person willing to host would be able to send an e-mail directly to the whole updated list, without having to send the e-mail to one person first like we used to do and without having to wonder if hitting "Reply All" is really getting the e-mail to everyone interested in being included.

To create a list serve, a congregation needs to sign up with a list serve website, which will host the list serve for a small monthly fee and provide the additional benefit of screening for spam. Someone still needs to be responsible for making sure the list serve is updated, but everyone can send e-mails to the list serve list without going through that one contact person each time.

Connections through Congregational Websites

Jacob's Well, a congregation in Kansas City, Missouri, created a community page on its website well before social networking sites such as Facebook and MySpace became popular. Individuals who want to sign up can create a profile including such things as the last book they read, their first job, and the address of their blog or Flickr page (a photo-sharing website). One of the playful aspects of the profile is to name the Star Wars character they identify with.

This portion of the congregation's website is very popular, and networking and online connection happen in a variety of ways through it. People can list the address of their home, and a map of the city shows where everyone lives. This enables people to engage in relationships in their neighborhood. The site includes a discussion area where anyone can start an online conversational ball rolling with any topic they desire to discuss.

When I tried to create an account on the Jacob's Well site, the site wasn't working correctly and I couldn't sign up. In a later conversation with a staff member at Jacob's Well, I learned that technical problems are not uncommon on the site. Most congregations cannot afford the complex software required to offer features like these. With the rise of social networking websites, a congregation might be better off setting up a group on one of those already established sites rather than trying to host a group on its own website.

More congregations and ministry organizations are establishing groups on Facebook, MySpace, Friendster, and Bebo. On these social networking websites, each group has a page where photos and other information can be posted. Often, the leaders of the congregation don't know who established the congregation's group on the site. Someone felt strongly enough about the significance of the congregation in his or her life to set up a way to connect with others who feel the same way.

Many ministers and rabbis have blogs, and many of them get a significant number of comments on blog posts. In some cases, the conversations among blog respondents function like online conversations, with one comment building on another.

A congregation in California has a place on its website to post anything that people want to give away, including things, time, and services. This portion of the website has proven to be very popular, and facilitates connections among congregation members in unexpected ways. All of these online connections illustrate the fluidity of the ways relationships are nurtured in our time, often with both face-to-face and online components.

Younger Generations and Online Community

I have talked with numerous men and women in their teens and twenties about how online community works for them. I will try to describe what I have learned, because I suspect that many people in older generations like me will find it quite different from the way we nurture relationships. And I suspect that relationships in the future will move more towards something like the model I am describing here.

Let's consider a twenty-four-year-old I will call Simon. Simon has a Facebook profile as well as a blog where he writes about politics and movies. His Facebook profile has a link to his blog.

Simon has had a Facebook profile for a couple of years, and over that time he has accumulated sixty-one "friends" on Facebook, both men and women. Several of them are people he knew in high school and college and with whom he remained in touch, so it was natural to find them on Facebook and connect with each other there. Several others are friends from childhood and high school with whom he had totally lost touch, but they reconnected through Facebook. A couple dozen of his Facebook friends are work colleagues, friends from his neighborhood, and people he knows from his church.

Some of Simon's Facebook friends are people he has never met in person but who are friends of his friends, and they got connected online because they had common interests in films and politics.

He met several of his other Facebook friends through blogging. Some of them write blogs he likes to read, and others have read Simon's blog and found him on Facebook.

Every day or two Simon updates his Facebook profile with his latest thoughts and activities, and all of his friends receive a notice about his updates. Likewise, he receives notice of his friends' updates to their profiles. If a friend is doing something interesting, Simon fires off a message to that friend using Facebook's e-mail capacity, which might result in a brief online exchange over the course of the day. It might also result in a social event that evening or during the next weekend.

Simon is in several groups on Facebook, including a group from his church. Sometimes he finds out about something interesting going on at church because of the Facebook group.

Simon loves blogging, and he reads dozens of blogs each week. He writes comments on some of them, often giving a link to his own blog, and sometimes those other bloggers read his blog posts and make comments. He experiences a sense of significant connection with some of those bloggers—including a few who have become Facebook friends—because he dialogues with them fairly intensely about politics and movies.

Simon's relationships flow seamlessly between the online and face-to-face environments. He attends a film discussion group at church, and many people in the group are his friends on Facebook and they continue the discussion of films through their Facebook posts. Sometimes the discussion of a film begins on Facebook on a blog post and results in an outing to see that film. Many of his Facebook friends and church friends read his blog, and they post their opinions and thoughts there. He lives several hundred miles from the town where he grew up, and when he plans a trip home, he uses his Facebook page and his blog to let his friends know he is coming so that he can see them in person.

Simon uses a variety of ways to stay connected to the people in his life. He sends numerous e-mails through his Facebook page, but he still uses his old e-mail address to stay in touch with people who aren't on Facebook. He has a cell phone and often sends text messages to arrange film outings as well as other social events with the group from church. He doesn't have a telephone land line anymore.

Simon's parents are quite concerned about all these online relationships. They wonder if all the people Simon meets online are actually honest about who they are. They worry that Simon will be tricked or manipulated by people faking their identity. Simon tosses off his parents' concerns. What does it matter, he asks, if he has a dialogue through Facebook or his blog with someone who is covering up his or her real identity? If the conversation is interesting, that's good enough.

And he would never arrange to meet a stranger anywhere private. The few times he has arranged to meet up with someone he met online, he always chooses a coffee shop as the location for that first meeting, and he chooses other public places for the second and third meetings as well. How is that any different from meeting a stranger at a cafe and arranging to meet up a second time, he wonders. Unscrupulous people can be anywhere, including the neighborhood or the workplace. We can have an interesting conversation with a shady person online or face-to-face. The same kinds of safeguards need to be in place.

Simon's pattern of relationships, flowing back and forth between online and face-to-face connections, is typical among the young people I have talked with, both men and women. In fact, "Simon" doesn't really exist. He is a composite of several people I interviewed. However, Simon's amazing number of social connections is not at all unusual among the people in their teens and twenties I talked with. His social contacts are often brief, often online, but no one can doubt that he is well-connected and involved both intellectually and socially with his friends.

Connections in a Postmodern Age

A century ago connections in a congregation took place in a formal way at the worship service and perhaps also at congregational din-

WIKIS: THE NEXT FRONTIER?

A wiki is software that allows people to create and edit documents on websites. The most famous wiki is Wikipedia, the online encyclopedia that allows viewers to make contributions to definitions, descriptions, and resources. Wikis are called "open source technology" because anyone accessing the site can contribute content; the source of the content is open to all.

Few congregations are currently using wikis, but they may become a helpful tool for congregations in the future. How might a congregation use a wiki?

An adult education class could use a wiki to create a statement about what they learned from the class. Members of the class could log on and write sentences and paragraphs that describe the topic of the class, while others might make corrections or suggestions. A group of people starting a new ministry might use a wiki to write their hopes, dreams, and plans for the ministry, and the document they create might later be used for publicity. The board of a congregation might use a wiki to create a document about a controversial issue, a building remodel or addition, or another challenge that they want to describe in a collaborative way to the congregation.

Contributions to a wiki are anonymous, unlike responses to blog posts or contributions to an online group. Lurkers are common on blogs and online groups because people are afraid of saying something stupid. A wiki might remove that fear, allowing people to make contributions more freely.

Wikis may prove to be one more way to affirm and experience unity and diversity, the value of multiple voices focused on a central purpose, one of the growing challenges of congregational life.

ners and other events. Because most congregations served specific parts of towns and cities, people from the congregation saw each other during the week in neighborhood shops and at community events. With the proliferation of the automobile and the growth of the suburbs in the second half of the twentieth century, the life of congregations became more isolated from everyday life. Congregation members had to create fellowship events in order to see each other, and congregation members were expected to structure their lives around the congregation's activities. That model worked for several decades largely because most women weren't working in careers outside the home and could make time for frequent congregational commitments.

Now people of faith have a renewed opportunity for multiple ways to connect, but that connection is not happening at neighborhood shops like it did one hundred years ago. Now those connections take place in the electronic neighborhood in such settings as congregational websites, blogs, online groups, list serves, and social networking websites. In the same way that the meetings in neighborhood shops a century ago were somewhat random and certainly not controlled by the congregation, so the opportunities for connection today have that same unstructured quality.

Connections in the postmodern era take place in multiple ways and a variety of places. They happen at odd times during the week, perhaps late at night, early in the morning, or during a coffee break at work. They often happen asynchronously; that is, a group of people can have a fairly intense connection with each other without being online at the same time.

Is this "real" community? It certainly feels real to me. At the same time, electronic communication cannot substitute for a hug, a sympathetic touch, or a warm smile. If congregational leaders promote various forms of online community, they will undoubtedly want to continue to promote forms of face-to-face community like small groups and neighborhood gatherings. The important emphasis to remember in this new environment is that online relationships and face-to-face relationships are not mutually exclusive. Often they nurture and support each other, creating a mosaic of relationships that connect and overlap in a variety of places and ways.

Online community can enhance face-to-face community and vice versa, as evidenced by the e-mail prayer requests and answers to prayer that circulated in my prayer support group and by the online map on the Jacob's Well website showing the location of people's homes. Simon and his friends meet in person to go to films and then they discuss them online, or they begin the discussion online and continue it in person. Online community can supplement congregational life in those situations where people's specific needs cannot be met in a congregation simply because others have not experienced the same trauma or specific challenge.

Among younger generations, engagement in community via the Internet is increasingly common, and online community connects seamlessly with everyday life. Congregational leaders can ignore this phenomenon or dive in unreservedly. They could also choose a middle ground, carefully learning about options for online community. They might begin by talking with younger people in the congregation to try to understand the ways younger people already engage in new forms of community and by asking their advice about how the congregation can participate in healthy and supportive ways.

A researcher on online religious community, Heidi Campbell, has found in several studies that online religious connections generally do not undercut congregational life. Most people who participate in online religious community are still involved in their local congregation. They simply view their online connections as a supplement to what they experience in the congregation.[1]

If community, relationships, and connections between people are valued in congregations, then the many faces of online community cannot be ignored. I have no doubts that by the time this book is printed, circulated, and read, new forms of electronic community will have emerged. New forms of digital community will raise new issues, and I hope that the discussion in this chapter will help to provide a framework for examining those new and emerging questions.

Whatever forms human connections take, we are driven by a deep-seated need to build and nurture relationships. I believe God created us that way, and I am not surprised by the many new ways people have found to connect in an electronic age.

Questions for Reflection, Journaling, and Discussion

1. Has the Internet facilitated any relationships for you? Did you have reservations at first? If so, what were they? What have you learned about online connections? What pros and cons of nurturing relationships online have you experienced?
2. If you are involved in an online group or a social networking website, what do you like about it? In what ways has it nurtured or impeded your life of faith?
3. If you are not involved in an online group or social networking website, who could you talk with about how they work, perhaps asking for a demonstration?
4. What do you see as opportunities for congregations in the area of online community? What do you see as pitfalls?

7 | The Gifts and Perils of Desktop Publishing

IMAGINE YOU ARE VISITING A CONGREGATION for the first time. You pick up a brochure about the congregation's upcoming mission trip. It's printed in a very casual, almost goofy, font, while the text lays out seven serious goals for the mission trip. Do the font and verbal text complement each other nicely, saying the trip will be both serious and fun? Or do they contradict each other?

Recently I came across an article in our local newspaper entitled, "What does your choice of typeface say about you?" The author, a journalist from a California newspaper, interviewed a handful of experts on typefaces who stressed some of the same things I learned in my six years as a desktop publisher. One of the first points the experts made is that typefaces are called fonts in most computer programs. Then they went on to talk about the significance of typefaces or fonts.

A typography analyst said, "Typefaces are the clothes words wear, and just as we make judgments about people by the clothes they wear, so we make judgments about the information we're reading by the typefaces." A creative director for an advertising agency reinforced the same idea: "The cliche in my business is that type talks. Think of it as your voice. A good company will be very consistent with its voice, whatever it's trying to convey. Some fonts are heavy and yell at you. Others are strong silent types."[1] These experts affirmed that sometimes the voice of the font speaks louder than the voice of the text.

A university researcher asked 561 people to apply adjectives to 20 popular fonts, and she came up with distinct personalities, both negative and positive, related to different typefaces. She reflected, "Typeface personalities do translate to the perception of the document."[2]

The Basics of Fonts

Fonts are divided into two main groups—serif and sans serif, which means without serifs. Serifs are the tiny horizontal lines added to the top and bottom of letters in fonts such as Times New Roman and Garamond. This book is printed in a serif font. Sans serif fonts lack those little lines and have a cleaner, simpler look. Examples of sans serif fonts are Arial and Verdana.

In the past, serif fonts were viewed as easier to read, so they were usually used for blocks of text, while sans serif fonts were often used for headlines because of their clean lines. In the 1950s and 1960s, sans serif fonts began to become more common in textbooks, so students educated in the 1960s and 1970s were increasingly comfortable with san serif fonts. As those students grew up, and some of them moved into design jobs, sans serif fonts became more common in magazines, brochures, advertisements, and other printed material. Web designers use sans serif fonts almost exclusively for blocks of text.[3]

In addition to the two major kinds of fonts, many cute and entertaining fonts have been created, some with spirals, stars, or other ornamentation. Others look like the text used in comic strips, on old typewriters, or on old computers. Script fonts that mimic handwriting or the typefaces used for traditional wedding invitations are also found on most computers. Many of these are hard to read and should be used sparingly so that readability can be maximized. In addition, these specialty fonts all have a much louder voice than the more common fonts, and that voice needs to be evaluated for its appropriateness as a companion for the message in the verbal text it is presenting.

EXAMPLES OF COMMON FONTS (OR TYPEFACES)

These are serif fonts:

Times New Roman

Garamond

Georgia

These are sans serif fonts:

Arial

Calibri

Verdana

These commonly used fonts do not have strong "voices" as fonts. Therefore they can be used frequently because they will not distract from the message conveyed by the words.

Font size also has significance. Font size is given in points, and 10, 11, or 12 points are the frequently used sizes for the body of text.[4] Ten-point font size is often a bit hard to read, particularly in the dim light of many worship spaces, so I always recommend using 12- or 13-point fonts for material designed to be read during worship. Subheads and headlines are usually in bigger fonts.

Two common mistakes frequently made by congregations illustrate the challenge of using fonts in the computer age. The first mistake is to print everything—weekly bulletins, newsletters, brochures—in the same font, using only one type size, with headers and headlines in all capital letters as if the document had been created on a typewriter. This makes publications look old-fashioned and out of touch with modern communication options, and the congregation is probably also perceived as out of date. The minimum requirement for a publication to look like it belongs to the twenty-first century is to use a larger font for headers and headlines and to minimize words in all capital letters.

The second mistake is more common. Many congregational publications look like advertisements for font designers, with a plethora of fonts in different sizes, sometimes in different colors that seem randomly applied. The rule of thumb in desktop publishing is to use only two fonts for each publication. A third font can perhaps be used in one or two places for emphasis, but introducing a third font and doing it well is difficult to do. I recommend that people don't try it unless they have had a lot of desktop publishing experience.

Fonts as Voices

If fonts are voices, then using multiple fonts in one publication usually means too many voices are saying different things. The constant challenge in congregational publications is to find a balance point where both unity and diversity are affirmed, and the diversity that is affirmed needs to reflect the diversity present in the congregation. Most often, when a multitude of fonts are used in a publication, the diverse voices of the fonts have nothing to do with reflecting the diversity within the congregation and instead simply convey confusion.

In the past, the two fonts used in a publication would usually be a serif font for the body of text and a sans serif font for the headlines. Desktop publishing and websites have changed this practice to some extent, and many attractive websites now use two or sometimes three sans serif fonts. Using two serif fonts in the same publication, online or in print, is difficult to do well.

In the article about fonts in my local newspaper, the experts all recommended a conservative approach for most publications,

HELVETICA

Helvetica is a sans serif font that has become common in advertising and signage. It is very similar to Arial. When I first started working as an editor and desktop publisher in 1990, I used Helvetica in its varying degrees of thickness for headlines and different headers and announcements. *Helvetica* is also the name of a feature-length documentary about the font, produced in 2007, the fiftieth anniversary of the typeface Helvetica's design. The documentary describes the typefaces common in the 1950s before Helvetica was designed and shows hundreds of examples of its ubiquitous use around the world. Interviews with graphic artists, typesetters, and printers—some of them enthusiastic about the font and others critical—help the viewer understand the ways that type affects our lives. The discussion and illustration in the documentary of this one common typeface is a wonderful way to learn about the broader issue of international visual culture.

This is Helvetica
This is Helvetica
This is Helvetica

so that the voice of the verbal text and graphics can communicate the message, rather than allowing the font to distract the reader or communicate something that contradicts the intended message. They advocated only occasional use of the specialty fonts and script fonts, both because they are harder to read and because they have such distinctive voices. They noted that using those specialty or script fonts for reports and correspondence tends to make the reader irritated because of the increased difficulty in reading the document.

The woman who conducted research linking personality traits to fonts said that those who want to come off well in reports and correspondence should stick with basic and familiar fonts, such as the serif fonts Times New Roman and Georgia and the sans serif fonts Verdana, Arial, and Calibri.

These same principles apply to most brochures, bulletins, newsletters, and websites produced by congregations. The body of text should be in one of those common, everyday fonts. Less common fonts can be used for headers and headlines, or perhaps for sidebars or small announcements, but the creators of the documents need to be careful what is communicated by each font. For example, an informal font paired with a formal font creates a sense of confusion, as if the congregation doesn't know who it is. (See sidebar on page 00 in chapter 1, "Fonts on Websites Speak.")

Common Desktop Publishing Mistakes

Each new release of word processing software over the past two decades has included more desktop publishing capabilities. Anyone using basic software now has access to an abundance of powerful tools for formatting text and placing photos and graphics. A generation ago these tools were available only to professional graphic artists. This wonderful opportunity to be creative with formatting words and images means that lots of wonderful—and awful—documents are being created.

The less attractive documents reflect poorly on the people and organizations who create them. A cluttered and visually jarring layout makes it hard to focus on what the words are saying. Because I love congregations and want the best for them, I want to help them use these powerful communication tools to convey the important and life-giving aspects of who they are and who God is in their midst.

So let's consider the common mistakes in congregational paper publications. The most common is to use too many fonts, creating a cluttered and confusing look, as if the congregation doesn't

READABILITY

Read these three brief paragraphs and watch your reading speed and comprehension. The first paragraph is in Arial, a common san serif font; the second paragraph is in Caflisch, a script font; and the third paragraph is Flowerpot, a more decorative font.

"Typefaces are the clothes words wear, and just as we make judgments about people by the clothes they wear, so we make judgments about the information we're reading by the typefaces." "Type talks. Think of it as your voice."

"Typefaces are the clothes words wear, and just as we make judgments about people by the clothes they wear, so we make judgments about the information we're reading by the typefaces." "Type talks. Think of it as your voice."

"Typefaces are the clothes words wear, and just as we make judgments about people by the clothes they wear, so we make judgments about the information we're reading by the typefaces." "Type talks. Think of it as your voice."

know who they are and what is most important to them. Other common mistakes include:

No Blank Space

Blank space on a page is the visual equivalent of taking a deep breath. If congregational communicators want to convey that their congregations are places of refuge in a frantic world, then careful use of white space is essential. Many congregational bulletins, brochures, and newsletters are crammed full of verbal text and graphics, conveying that an overloaded life is an unavoidable part of the journey of faith.

Clip Art That Appears Random

Clip art works well when it complements the verbal text or when it conveys something significant about a congregation's identity. Too often, clip art in congregational publications looks like it was chosen at random, perhaps to convey cheerful friendliness or perhaps because of fear of having blank space. Random clip art conveys a message that this congregation doesn't really know who they are or what they value, but they want to be cheerful in their lack of direction.

Columns That Are Too Wide

Newspapers throughout history have used narrow columns for a reason. They are easier to read. Text that goes across a whole page is hard to read, especially when it is single spaced. Research shows that columns wider than sixty-five characters slows reading speed and comprehension. Columns are so easy to create in word processing software today that there is no excuse to use text that goes across an entire page. When I struggle through a newsletter that uses one too-wide column, I feel like the creators of the newsletter don't care about me and my needs.

Extra-Small Fonts

In an attempt to fit in more text, the editor or designer find it all too easy to put text in 8 or 9 points, which is simply too small for most readers. Many seniors are most comfortable with 12- or 13-point type for blocks of text. Very small type conveys the message that the people creating this publication were too lazy to edit the text or too cheap to pay for the printing of another page. Older readers may also feel that the creators of the publication are insensitive to their needs.

Ignoring the Possibility of More Space between Lines

Early word processing programs offered the option of single, double, or triple spacing. Then the option of one-and-a-half spaces came along. Now any line spacing is possible in word processing programs, as has always been the case in desktop publishing software. Adding extra spacing between lines of text can open up text, making it easier to read and sometimes conveying a feeling of peace or serenity. If a community of faith wants to communicate that it provides a place of refuge in God in a world gone mad with activities and consumption, using text with extra space between the lines can make a small contribution in communicating that peace.

Overuse of Capital Letters, Bold, and Italics

Capital letters, bold, and italics make text stand out. They also slow down reading speed. Therefore they should be used only occasionally. In the age of desktop publishing, either bold or italics—but not both at the same time—is the preferred way to make text stand out. But use bold and italics only for occasional emphasis. A whole paragraph in bold or italics decreases readability dramatically. Words in capital letters should be used very, very sparingly.

Seemingly Random Use of Color

In the same way that capital letters, bold, and italics make text stand out, so does color. The careful use of color can highlight a word or an idea and increase comprehension in readers. But using colored text well is difficult, particularly when more than one color is used. As with clip art, seemingly random use of color can communicate a lack of coherence in a publication.[5]

Using Photos and Graphics in Newsletters

Congregational newsletters reflect the competence and interests of the people who create them, and part of the joy of life in congregations is the way people's personalities shine through the things they do. Based on looking at dozens of church newsletters, I would hazard a guess that some of the people who create newsletters love clip art, others love photos, and others are a bit uncomfortable with adding anything to words.

Because I have visited so many congregations, I can say with confidence that photos of the congregational staff in newsletters are very helpful, particularly if that staff person is writing an article or leading an upcoming event. Reading an article by a staff member and wondering if I have seen that person or not is frustrating. Photos of lay leaders who have written an article are also helpful. On the other hand, if the only picture in a newsletter month after month is the minister, then the newsletter is communicating nonverbally that the minister is the central focus of the congregation.

For visitors, photos that give a flavor of life in this congregation are also helpful. They can provide a window into the congregation's activities and help new people feel less awkward about joining in, because the visitors can visualize what it would look like.

The purpose of clip art and photos in newsletters is worthy of careful consideration by congregational leaders and newsletter editors so that the unique priorities of the congregation can be reflected in the visual appearance of the newsletter. Is the purpose of clip art and photos to fill empty space? To add visual beauty? To provide a snapshot of congregational life? To affirm the people who plan and lead events? To help newcomers find a place to get involved? To make sure congregation members know their staff and leaders? To recruit for events and programs? To make the congregation feel good about itself?

These are all reasons to use photos and clip art. Wise use of these resources will come from careful thinking and discussion so that a variety of opinions can be honored.

Meeting the Needs of Visitors and Newcomers

If a congregation values reaching out to the community and helping new people feel welcome, then those values will have implications for the congregation's newsletter. Before being printed, every edition of a congregational newsletter should be read, at least once, through the eyes of someone who knows nothing about the congregation.

Common errors include not identifying the people who write the articles. First-time visitors and people who are fairly new to the congregation don't know the names of people in the congregation. If Susan Smith is a congregational leader or on the staff, then her role should be put beside her name as the author of the article. If someone in the congregation writes an article, then a short bio should be given at the end of the article: "Josh Jones is a Christ Church member who serves on the outreach committee." If the person's profession is relevant to the topic of the article, it should be noted. For example, an article about the renovations of the education wing might say at the end: "Harry Wang is a local building contractor who serves on our construction committee."

The use of jargon, insider information, and acronyms are other common newsletter errors that make visitors and newcomers feel that they don't belong. I can't tell you how often I have visited a church and read an announcement in the bulletin or newsletter like this: "FRM meets this Wednesday evening at the Wilsons'. All are welcome." What is FRM? Where do the Wilsons live? Why should I consider attending? Who would I contact if I want more information? How would I contact that person? When I read announcements like that, I feel unwanted and unwelcome.

Perhaps the people hosting an event don't want their addresses and phone numbers in the newsletter. In that case, the notice about the event can say something like, "For more information, contact Andrew Adams, Lilydale Lutheran's administrative assistant, at . . ." Paying attention to these kinds of details will help make the newsletter more newcomer friendly.

The Voice in Newsletters

Who gets to speak in a congregation's newsletter? Is the minister the only person with a byline? Do congregation members know how to submit items for the newsletter?

A minister who has served numerous churches as an interim told me that congregation members seldom have much ownership for newsletters or websites. They often don't know how submissions are chosen. The process is mysterious, and the power behind the newsletter is hidden or assumed to belong to the minister or secretary.

Congregational newsletters should have a clear statement in every issue of how to submit news items and articles and what the deadline for each issue is. If the articles are all written by one person, then others may need to be asked to write brief articles in order to show that the newsletter is democratic and not dominated by one voice.

I recommend that an editorial board of two or three people be chosen and their names be listed in each issue of the newsletter so that a group of people is making decisions about newsletter content. This keeps voices of criticism from falling too strongly on one person, and it begins the process of congregational ownership of the newsletter.

One challenge with newsletters is the same as with all congregational communication: how to affirm both unity and diversity. The unity of the congregation can be affirmed by the consistent use of the same logo or slogan, by a column every month by staff members or leaders, and by a consistent and coherent format.

The diversity can be affirmed through articles written by different members, articles describing multiple congregational ministries, or through photos of various individuals or activities.

Adapting Newsletters to Websites

Congregations typically adopt one of three strategies for posting information from paper newsletters onto websites. Some congregations scan their printed newsletter to create a PDF file or save the newsletter in PDF.[6] The PDF file is then posted on the website, and website viewers can download the PDF file and read it using Adobe Reader.

Other congregations take the articles from the newsletter and post them on the website as web pages. Sometimes each article has its own page and sometimes the whole newsletter has a web page. The material from the newsletter is clearly identified as coming from the newsletter, so the link usually says something like "March newsletter" or "most recent newsletter." These first two ways of posting newsletters make it easy to create a file of past newsletters, with a link to newsletters for each month or week.

A third approach is for the newsletter material to be adapted for website use in such a way that the website viewer has no idea the material came from a newsletter. The links describe the content of the articles rather than noting the material came from a newsletter. The articles and announcements from the newsletter may be shortened.

The first strategy takes the least amount of time and labor and is most common in small congregations without a lot of money or people power for updating the website. The third strategy is most common in large congregations with full-time staff who keep up with websites.

All three strategies work. However, reading PDF files can be irritating for three reasons. First, it takes time for the files to download. Second, PDF files on websites are usually a bit blurry.

Third, if the newsletter layout uses more than one column, which is a good idea to increase readability, and if the columns are long, then they will probably extend below the screen when the PDF version of the newsletter is downloaded. This requires the reader to scroll back up to the top of the page after reading the left-hand column, an action that takes time and is not a natural action on a website. Therefore, if the resources are available, I encourage congregations to post newsletter articles as web pages rather than PDF files.

However, newsletters posted on websites as PDF files are far better than nothing. For people who want information about a congregation and for members who are trying to track down a detail in the past, having past and present newsletters on the website is very helpful. In a congregation where web resources are limited, using material from the newsletter is a way to keep the website updated at least once a month and to provide a lot of information about the congregation.

More congregations are sending their newsletters as e-mails, either weekly or monthly, and I would encourage those congregations to post their e-mailed newsletters on their websites as well. Newsletters contain all sorts of valuable information, and it is a pity to lose that information, when posting them on the website is easy to do.

Welcome Brochures

A simple, clear brochure that expresses a few of the basic characteristics of the congregation is a simple and effective tool to help newcomers feel welcome and receive some basic information about the congregation. The brochure should have the following components:

- The congregation's name, address, phone, and website
- The names and contact information of some or all staff
- The names and contact information of one or more lay leaders

- A brief description of the congregation's worship style
- The time of worship services if they stay fairly constant
- Some information on what is available for children and youth
- A brief overview of the ministries of the congregation
- The denominational affiliation, if any
- Something about what makes this congregation unique: its values, particular emphases, history, location, style of outreach, or special ministries
- Brief descriptions of the congregation's history and priorities might be included. A slogan or logo can give visitors a way to remember the congregation. One or two photos of congregational activities gives visitors a window into the congregation.

The congregation's welcome brochure and website should use similar text, graphics, fonts, and photos. They don't need to be identical, but they should definitely not be totally different. The feel of the layout does not need to be identical, because the web medium and paper publications are distinctly different. But the website and the brochure should have some similarities in layout.

The welcome brochure and the website are the two major places where newcomers get basic, general information about the congregation. They need to be examined side-by-side to be sure that they are presenting views of the congregation that do not contradict each other. When I visited so many congregations a few years ago, I was amazed at the disparities between what congregations said about themselves in printed publications and on their websites.

The Gift of Desktop Publishing

If a person or congregation can afford a computer and some software, then they have access to powerful tools that used to be available only to professional graphic designers. These tools have raised the bar for everyone. Messy or careless letters, handouts, fliers, newsletters, and brochures speak strongly about the values of the people who created them or the institutions they represent. Publications that look outdated seem to say that the people or institutions who created them are outdated.

The potential for excellence as well as mediocrity creates a need for humility and careful study on the part of the people who create congregational publications. Learning the basic principles about desktop publishing will go a long way toward making publications speak of the congregation's values more clearly. With desktop publishing, simplicity and clarity are always good goals.

Questions for Reflection, Journaling, and Discussion

1. Do you agree that fonts speak? Can you think of an example where a font effectively reflected or did not reflect the verbal text it was expressing?

2. Write a sentence in a word processing program, then copy and paste it fifteen times, and put each sentence in a different font. Enlarge all the sentences to 24-point font size. Print the page with the sentence in all the different fonts. Try to assign adjectives to each of the fonts (bold, casual, formal, friendly, and so forth). This exercise will help you begin to understand the voices of fonts.

3. What are the characteristics of the best congregational newsletter you have ever seen? What do you think are the strengths and weaknesses of your congregation's newsletter?

4. Does your congregation have a welcome brochure? Imagine yourself as a visitor to your congregation. Does the brochure answer all your questions?

5. Lay out on a table your congregation's welcome brochure, website, worship folder, and newsletter. In what ways do

they present a coherent picture of your congregation? In what ways do they seem to present different pictures? Do those different pictures complement or contradict each other?

8 | Two Controversial Tools

Mission Statements and Projection Screens

BILL IS ONE OF THOSE LUCKY INDIVIDUALS with a genetic predisposition to slenderness. For most of his life he stayed thin, despite his love for junk food and smoking and his distaste for regular exercise. When he hit forty, his bad habits caught up with him and he gained a few pounds.

His wife, his close friend, and his physician had been telling him for years that his health was at risk, and they stepped up their pressure when he started gaining weight. So Bill cut back the quantities of pizza, chips, and beer; lost the few pounds; and smugly told them they could stop nagging any time.

Bill continued to eat junk food, smoke, and sit around without exercising. In some ways he was better off with the few extra pounds, because then he had visible feedback from the mirror that his health needed attention. Bill's slender body made him look healthy, but his health was deceptive.

I have saved two seemingly unrelated congregational communication tools—mission statements and projection screens—for this penultimate chapter because they are like Bill after he lost a few pounds. They look good, and they can make congregational leaders feel they have done their job in the area of communication.

Mission statements can be a part of a discernment process in which congregational leaders seek to hear God's voice about who the congregation is called to be and what it is called to do. I applaud anything that encourages leaders to listen to God's direction. However, it appears to me that mission statements often become bland, all-inclusive statements that communicate almost nothing. And they are often so long that they can't be used in brochures or on the home pages of websites, so they seldom get used. In addition, the presence of the mission statement can lull congregational leaders into complacency about their task of assessing and determining direction for the congregation. An existing mission statement can make leaders feel they have adequately discussed their sense of God's call, while, I believe, discerning God's call is an ongoing process requiring continued prayer and discernment.

Congregations may be better off without mission statements. When a congregation has no mission statement, its leaders are more likely to realize they need to spend time considering how best to communicate the priorities of the congregation in a brief and appealing way.

My concern about screens and video (or data) projectors in worship appears on the surface to be different from my concern about mission statements. However, the two concerns have similarities. My observation is that the text and graphics on screens in worship are often poorly done. The words of the songs appear out of order, announcements use every possible font and color and therefore appear disorienting and chaotic, and sermons are illustrated with countless bullet points and lists that are distracting at best, while at worst they oversimplify the richness of our faith traditions.

In addition, screens are mesmerizing, and I worry that the text and visuals on screens, whether well or poorly done, can keep people focused on the screen rather than on worshiping God. So in that regard, my concern about screens has parallels with my concern about mission statements. I worry that both of them can be impediments to engaging with the living God in a posture of reverence and receptivity.

In one additional area, a congregation may be better off without a screen. When a congregation doesn't have a projection screen but wants to make its worship more visual, its leaders will realize they need to think creatively about how to do that. Congregations that use screens are more likely to believe their worship service is already visual enough.

In this chapter I will present the pros and cons of these two tools. I will express my own reservations about their use as well as the reservations I have read and heard about, but I will present several of the arguments in favor of their use as well.

Mission Statements

A group of congregational leaders wants to communicate more clearly what its congregation values, what the congregation focuses on, and where it is headed. The leaders gather for prayer and reflection over many months, trying to discern God's voice about these issues. After numerous meetings, they come up with a mission statement that describes the congregation.

The statement is concise, clear, and focused. The congregation begins using the statement in its worship folder, in its newsletter, and on its website. The statement brings unity to the congregation's publications and provides a focus for the congregation's ministries. Newcomers to the congregation find the statement helpful, and members are happy to have a statement that so well describes who they are. The statement communicates both where the congregation is now and where it is headed, so members, newcomers, and visitors have a sense of where this congregation might be in a few years. The statement gives everyone a sense of peace and vision.

Is this a fiction? Do mission statements ever work that well? Yes, in some cases they do. And those cases are just frequent enough to keep mission statements on the radar screen for congregational leaders.

Gil Rendle and Alice Mann, in *Holy Conversations: Strategic Planning as a Spiritual Practice for Congregations*, argue that mission statements can be a helpful step in the strategic planning process for congregations. For Rendle and Mann, creating a mission statement comes near the end of a prayerful process of discernment of vision that involves "reading" the congregation's culture and the community setting: "Clarity comes from our conversations about who we are, what biblical stories shape us, what memories of congregational life we cling to, what values we most want to carry with us, what geographic and human areas we have been called to serve, and what our community needs from us."[1] These considerations are all factors that will shape a mission statement, which they define simply as a "statement of identity and purpose."[2]

Rendle and Mann note two components of mission statements: the axiomatic and the unique. The axiomatic describes values that are shared by all congregations or by all congregations with a common denominational heritage. Rendle and Mann cite an example that illustrates axiomatic beliefs and practices: "Third United Methodist Church of Anytown is called to serve both members and the wider community through worship, the administration of the sacraments, Christian education, acts of caring, and outreach."[3] This statement summarizes the core activities of this congregation and thousands of other churches as well.

Unique aspects of a mission statement focus on the values that the congregation embraces. These unique components might reflect the congregation's focus on an outreach to homeless people, a strong commitment to overseas missions, an embrace of the visual arts, an emphasis on well-performed traditional church music, a cafe-style worship service, or countless other distinct activities. When Rendle and Mann consult with congregations involved in a visioning process, they encourage them to center their mission statements on these unique aspects of the congregation. They have found that these components stimulate the energy the congregation needs to move confidently into the future. They also encourage the congregation not to stop the visioning process with the creation of a mission statement, but instead move on to creating objectives, goals, and recommendations that flow out of the visioning process and the mission statement.

The Origin of Mission Statements

To understand some of the issues around the current use of mission statements, it is helpful to consider their origin and use in the business world. Mission statements became common in the corporate world in the 1980s at the urging of Peter Drucker and other business consultants who promoted mission statements as a way for companies to articulate their highest purpose. About 85 percent of large companies currently have them. Can you identify the companies represented by these mission two statements? "To enable people and businesses throughout the world to realize their full potential." "Organize the world's information and make it universally accessible and useful."

These two mission statements come from Microsoft and Google, respectively. Microsoft's mission statement is lofty and expansive and could apply to hundreds or even thousands of businesses. Its mission statement is a good illustration of a statement that says almost nothing—but in an inspiring way—and could be considered pabulum or a platitude. Google's statement focuses more precisely on what the company actually does.

In the past two decades, congregations have followed the business world and adopted mission statements as a way to articulate who they are and what they value. One of the objections to mission statements in congregations comes from their origin in the business world. How much should congregations adopt techniques and strategies that originate in corporations?

A second objection comes from the way mission statements have evolved in businesses. All too often they are so general that they communicate very little about the unique focus of the business. In a 2007 *New York Times* article on mission statements, an expert is quoted as saying that fewer than 10 percent of corporate mission statements say anything meaningful about the company.[4] Something similar could probably be said of congregational mission statements.

The *New York Times* article points out that in some businesses the process of coming up with the mission statement is very helpful for the employees or owners who work on it. And a mission statement has helped companies discern new vision or evaluate the way they work. The same can be said for congregations. In some cases, mission statements have proven to be valuable.

Contemporary Communication of Identity

In the twenty-first century, identity is constructed and communicated through an assemblage of words and images, connections and actions. Earlier in this book I cited the example of a congregation with a brief and effective mission statement that it used on the home page of its website. Unfortunately, the web designer had chosen an extremely casual, goofy font for the mission statement, which was juxtaposed with the name of the congregation in an elegant script font. The name of the church and the mission statement were the two main components on the congregation's home page.

The congregation's identity was communicated on that home page as much by the fonts that were chosen as by the name and mission statement of the congregation. In fact, the contradictory message communicated by the fonts spoke just as loudly as the words did.

Congregations often believe that once they have gotten their mission statement in place, they are then free from needing to spend energy considering the ways they communicate who they are. However, in the twenty-first century, in this era of so many varied communication technologies, the task of identity construction never really ends. Congregations can embrace this task as a part of the vital process of discerning God's direction. Or they can ignore it, and as a result their communication will probably be random and unfocused.

One challenge with mission statements in our time is that most mission statements are simply too long to use on the home pages of websites and blogs or on congregational brochures and bulletins.

A slogan-length statement is appropriate for twenty-first-century communication media, something four to fifteen words long. And a visual component alongside the slogan, such as a congregational logo, makes the slogan memorable.

A recent comment by my husband illustrates this reality. We were talking about congregational mission statements, and he said, "The one I remember the best is that church we visited that used a tree. They had a large wood bas-relief sculpture of the tree in their entrance, and they used the tree on all their brochures and on the Sunday bulletin. The mission statement said something about a tree."

After talking with my husband, I checked that congregation's website. The tree appeared in numerous places on the website with "Isaiah 61:3" nestled in the roots of the tree. The verse from Isaiah contains the words, "They will be called oaks of righteousness, the planting of the LORD, to display his glory," and the congregation had decided to adopt that visual image as a kind of slogan for the congregation. The result was something that my husband remembered more than two years after we had visited that congregation just one time.

Another illustration of an effective slogan comes from a congregation I attended years ago. It has a lengthy mission statement that is used at times by the staff and lay leaders to evaluate the congregation's ministries. I am not sure if many members of the church know the statement exists, and I couldn't find it on the congregation's website. The leaders of that congregation have taken one idea out of the mission statement to use as a slogan: "Every member a minister."[5]

The slogan appears frequently in congregational publications and spoken communication. The concept of every member engaging in ministry shapes the congregation's activities, planning, communication, preaching, and worship. Leaders have done an excellent job choosing a slogan that fits the ethos of the church and that shapes the church's ministry choices.

Of the sixty-six church websites I studied for my dissertation, around one-quarter used some sort of slogan, a brief statement posted close to the church's name on the website. Some of these slogans relate to the churches' mission statements, which may be posted on the home page or elsewhere on the website. Other slogans seem to be chosen to convey something of the congregation's unique emphasis.

Some slogans seek to describe the congregation as a place:

- Community in the heart of the city[6]
- The little church with a really big heart[7]
- Sacred space for the city[8]
- A place to get connected[9]
- A harbor of hope[10]
- A place to encounter God together and become fully devoted to worshiping him[11]
- An open and affirming church, a spirited justice-seeking community[12]
- A modern first-century church[13]

Other slogans focus on what the church does or hopes to do:

- Connecting people to God[14]
- Caring for each other, embracing the world[15]
- To know God, to grow in faith, to show God's love[16]
- Loving God, loving people[17]
- Transforming ordinary people into extraordinary followers of Christ[18]

Four to fifteen words isn't enough to say much about a congregation, but it does give a slice of the congregation's focus and can be welcoming and inviting.

Mission statements, slogans, and logos are a part of how congregations communicate who they are and what they value, but in an age of patchworked identity composed of many verbal, visual, and participatory elements, they are only a part. They need to be viewed in the context of all the ways a congregation communicates, as one component, not even a central component.

Projection Screens in Worship

A second contemporary communication tool that can be overemphasized is the screen for data projection. I have seen numerous examples of effective use of screens in worship. For example, in 2005, a couple of weeks after Hurricane Katrina, I was visiting a congregation that uses a screen in its worship service. About ten minutes into the service, after a few announcements, an opening hymn and an opening prayer, an array of images of New Orleans under water were shown.

While one image after another appeared on the screen, a cellist played mournful music softly in the background, and the worship leader read an assortment of verses from the Bible about water. The slideshow of images was immediately followed by a long and heartfelt prayer for the people of New Orleans.

Tears filled my eyes as I entered into the prayer. Because of the careful use of images of the flooding, I prayed for people affected by the hurricane in a new and deep way. In addition, the combination of the visuals, the sad music, and the Scripture verses communicated to me in an experiential way that God cared deeply for the people there and desired my prayers for the situation.

A second example comes from a congregation with a breakfast outreach service that meets in a school auditorium. The minister of the congregation befriended the school's custodian, who cleaned and set up the auditorium before and after the service. This custodian is an enthusiastic bonsai gardener, and in several conversations with the minister, the custodian explained how to create a bonsai tree.

As the minister listened to the custodian talking about the significance of clipping the roots of trees and giving them shallow soil, he was struck by the parallels to the life of faith and biblical passages such as Psalm 1 and John 15. The minister asked the custodian if he would be willing to come to the worship service and talk about the art of bonsai. The custodian said no.

So the minister asked the custodian if he would be willing to be videotaped talking about bonsai. No problem, said the custodian. So the minister videotaped a conversation, did some editing, and showed the videotape in worship as a part of a sermon on growing deep roots in Christ. The video seemed to the minister to be an effective illustration of the issues connected with the sermon, and he got feedback from members of the congregation indicating their appreciation for that visual illustration.

The video had a completely unexpected benefit. Families in the congregation who had children in the school at that time now often strike up conversations with the custodian. Because of seeing him in a video explaining his love of bonsai, they feel they know him and can talk casually with him.

A third example comes from a congregation where the youth group wrote and produced a brief video about "Bible Boy," a superhero who bashed people verbally (and physically a few times as well) with the Bible. The video did a good job presenting appropriate and inappropriate use of the Bible. The video was shown in the Sunday worship service during the children's time. The youth group members were proud of their contribution, the adults got to know the youth a little better, and the younger children were utterly fascinated.

And Yet

Those stories might make it seem obvious that congregations would want to use video projectors routinely in worship. After all, it saves significant money and trees not to print the words of the songs and prayers every week or to buy hymnbooks, but instead show them on the screen. And who can deny the appropriateness of projecting the words to Scripture readings at the same time those words are read? Video projectors and screens provide an opportunity to highlight the creative efforts of people in the congregation. And if a picture paints a thousand words, then why would congregations miss an opportunity to paint those words and enhance their communication of God's truth and love?

A VISUAL FOCUS WITHOUT A SCREEN

Is it possible for a congregation to embrace the visually oriented, image-driven nature of today's global culture without using a screen in worship? Two Protestant congregations representing opposite ends of the theological spectrum would emphatically answer yes.

One of them, an evangelical congregation, has a large number of people in their twenties, thirties, and forties. The congregation's arts group enables a strong focus on the visual arts. Two rooms in the church are equipped with rails mounted near the ceiling from which rotating art displays are hung on picture wire. In addition, two or three times a year the group asks artists within the congregation to contribute to a specific art project. Several times members of the group have created large charcoal drawings that were hung on the walls of the sanctuary for Lent, Advent, or Pentecost. Several other times members of the group have created installations that speak of Christian values. One of those was a collection of doors decorated by artists that stood on the church's front lawn to indicate the welcome of Jesus. In addition, in some seasons of the year, artists in this congregation, both adults and children, supply line drawings for the cover of worship bulletins.

A second congregation, a liberal mainline congregation, has large murals on the walls of its sanctuary depicting the life of saints and heroes of faith. The sanctuary is also decorated with art objects from around the world, such as Ethiopian crosses and Japanese origami cranes. In addition, the ministers and lay people leading services dress in robes made of bright African cloth.

The visual emphasis at the first congregation draws on the artists within the congregation with rotating art displays. The second draws on permanent art and a global perspective. Neither congregation uses a projection screen for worship, but the congregations' rich visual focus affirms the significance of the visual arts and speaks of their values as a congregation.

At the same time, the use of data projectors and screens can also be problematical. In the same church where the youth group showed the video, on the Sunday before the video was shown, the technicians had a hard time getting the video projector going at the beginning of the service. The first two songs were sung without the congregation having access to the words. Only a few people in the congregation knew the songs, the congregation doesn't have hymnbooks in the pews, and the worship team that week was composed mostly of musicians who don't sing. As a result, during those first two songs only a few people sang, and it was impossible to hear the melody or make out the words. As a worship experience, those two songs were a nonevent.

When the data projector isn't working, how long do you wait to begin the service? What does the congregation do when the technicians are scrambling around trying to figure out what's wrong? When the data projector in a worship space is new, it is easy to come to every worship service with a backup plan, but after the projector works a few dozen times, it is easy to be lulled into the complacency of believing it will always work.

Another challenge related to the use of screens is the distinctly different ways visual messages are perceived by worshipers. Some people are highly sensitive to visual cues and seldom watch television and movies because the images remain in their mind. For those people, to be barraged by visual information during worship is highly distracting and even draining.

Many congregations use their screens to display a rotating list of announcements. Often these announcements are displayed before the service starts. Some people are able to read them once and then tune them out. Other people find the constantly changing screen makes it hard to pray in those moments before worship. I worry that displaying announcements on a screen before worship encourages passive screen watching rather than active prayer and reflection in order to prepare for worship.

Some congregations display the rotating list of announcements while the verbal announcements are being made. People who enjoy that practice have told me that everyone multitasks

PROPS: A VISUAL FOCUS
WITHOUT A SCREEN

One minister has a brocade robe he wears for particular sermons. The robe signals the congregation that he will be engaging in a different kind of sermon, a role play where he acts the part of a biblical character who dialogues with a character from life today. Another minister works hard to figure out props that provide illustrations for his sermon. For a sermon on service, using the metaphor of foot washing, he brought a foot bath onto the platform, took off his shoes and socks, and got his feet wet. Another time, when preaching on the Incarnation, he held a congregation member's baby during the first part of the sermon.

In the research by *Leadership Journal* cited in this chapter, one-third of the ministers surveyed reported using more props than they used to. Props make sermons visual in a low-tech way that can seem authentic to the congregation. Props help children engage in worship, and perhaps the child in all of us delights to see a well-chosen prop. The only sermon I remember from the first eighteen years of my life focused on fulfilling one's purpose. The minister had a watch that was no longer working, and he threw it into the congregation to illustrate its uselessness. I will never forget that watch flying overhead. Props bring a light-heartedness to worship that communicates the values of humor as well as relevance.

these days, so it makes sense to have announcements presented visually and verbally at the same time, even if different events are being announced simultaneously, one orally and one visually. I find this practice overwhelming, irritating, and incongruous with the worship of God. The confusion and overstimulation of messages on a screen that differ from the verbal announcements seem to contradict the message that God is the source of peace, joy, and quality of life. Furthermore, neuroscientists tell us that people can't really multitask. We will always attend to one thing at the expense of the other.[19]

Some Research on Screens

Leadership Journal conducted research into the rise in the use of screens and visual components during worship.[20] They surveyed 515 subscribers to the journal, all of whom are senior ministers who preach frequently. They found that 73 percent of the churches used a screen or other visual component in worship. More than half of the ministers reported that their use of PowerPoint had increased in the past three years. Half of the ministers reported using more multimedia clips from movies, TV, or other sources during worship. One-third used more videos made by church staff or members.

Smaller congregations and liturgical churches were less likely to use video and screens, but, according to the research, these gaps are not as great as they once were. For example, half of the smallest churches used more technology than they did a few years ago. In all the churches sampled, the most common uses of screens were functional rather than artistic, with 92 percent of the churches using screens for song lyrics. Other common uses were announcements, sermon points, and Scripture readings. Photographic and artistic images are increasingly used, but they are not projected nearly as frequently as song lyrics, announcements, sermon points, and Scripture readings.

In 72 percent of the congregations represented in the *Leadership Journal* survey, volunteers operated the worship technologies. However, paid audiovisual staff members are becoming more common in churches of all sizes as the technology becomes more complex and time consuming.

An additional use of screens is common in very large churches, where the speaker's image can be projected on a screen large enough so that people sitting further back can see the speaker's facial expressions. When people hear about this strategy, they often find it distasteful, but for many who attend these large congregations, it feels natural and helpful.

All of these statistics and trends seem to indicate that soon almost all congregations will use screens. However, it is noteworthy that some congregations attracting younger members are moving away from screens and embracing even more participatory forms of worship. One increasingly common practice is the use of stations around the room where worshipers can go to receive prayer or communion, have their feet washed, light a candle and pray for a family member, write their sins on a piece of paper and burn it, draw their interpretation of a Scripture passage, or engage in other forms of active worship.

The Roman Catholic and Eastern Orthodox churches have a long tradition of multisensory worship with a strong visual focus. As more Protestant Christians are learning from these two traditions, many visual aspects of worship—without a screen—can be incorporated into patterns of worship that were originally not visual.

New Uses of Screens

Congregations with younger members are likely to view screens during worship as a way to help create a worship environment. The screen is used to project the words of songs, but for the rest of the service the screen plays a role, along with other visual and sensory components, in the making of a place where worship can happen. In the past, stained-glass windows and architecture played a part in this sensory creation of a worship space, and now the screen does the same with photos of art or nature, or video or movie clips.

In congregations with younger members, screens might be used during sermons to display a medieval painting on a topic related to the sermon, a photo that illustrates a metaphor used in the sermon, or a quotation relevant to the sermon's topic that might not be read aloud by the preacher. A preacher in his thirties who often uses the screen to post quotations related to his sermon said, "If people don't want to listen, they can read the quotation and ignore me." He believes the sermon is an experience and he tries to find visuals and quotations that will illustrate the story he is telling and enhance the experience of being there for the sermon. He is emphatic that he does not want to use the screen to "dump knowledge" on the people listening to his sermon; instead, he wants to use images that tell a story or provoke questions.

One congregation encourages worshipers to use their cell phones to send text message questions about the sermon, and the technician collects the questions and posts them on the screen so that everyone can see what questions have emerged from the sermon. This strategy shows the move away from tightly scripted sermons with a bullet point for every idea to an increasingly participatory form of worship.

Film and TV clips are increasingly common in worship, particularly as illustrations for sermons. The challenge with finding clips is to walk a fine line between engaging and exciting. A clip that is too exciting will overshadow the message of the sermon. Film and TV clips can easily be too long; three minutes is usually long enough. As one minister said, "It's a church service, not a Christian film discussion." Some congregations find it works best to use the version of films that have the words displayed along the bottom of the screen so that everyone can get the words.

PowerPoint

Many people in younger generations are not fond of the use of screens to display outlines or bullet points during sermons. PowerPoint as a presentation style with its bullet-point lists and short, pithy summaries is generally viewed as a baby boomer phenomenon. Authenticity is increasingly important in congregational life, and it doesn't appear authentic to some people to have words on a screen that exactly parallel the words the preacher is saying.

MAKING WORDS VISUAL

The linguistic version of images is stories and metaphors. As global culture becomes more visual, stories and metaphors are becoming more significant in verbal communication, both written and oral. Stories have always played an important role in preaching, but often those were stories of other people in other places. Stories that seem to communicate well in our time are personal stories that illustrate God's work in the life of the person telling the story.

One congregation has a slot at the end of each worship service called, "What my faith means to me." Anyone in the congregation can get up and tell a brief story about God's work in his or her life, and almost every Sunday someone experiences a nudge to tell a story. In another congregation, the annual meeting each year features half a dozen personal testimonies of the way God worked in people's lives in the past year; each person was asked by the minister ahead of time to tell a piece of his or her story. In another congregation, photos of people on the home page of the congregational website are actually links to each person's faith story.

Metaphors are another way of bringing visual impact into spoken or written words. The Bible is full of metaphors: God is our rock, fortress, and shepherd, Jesus is the light of the world and the bread of life, to mention only a few. Modern-day metaphors abound as well: the home as an oasis, friends and family as a sanctuary, work as slavery, again to mention only a few. Metaphors will play an increasingly important role in verbal communication as global culture continues to become more visual.

Highly scripted presentations with elaborate PowerPoint backup seem canned and rehearsed and not from the heart.

A video or data projector can show whatever is on a computer screen: a website, a word processing document, a database, a video, or anything else. PowerPoint is used because the software enables people to put objects in frames that exactly fit a computer screen. Therefore, when the view on the screen is projected, the entire image or verbal text is displayed. Nothing is invisible, nothing is outside the screen's limits.

Photos, charts, and other visual components can be loaded onto PowerPoint slides and projected sequentially onto a screen, just like an old-fashioned slide show. But PowerPoint can also be used as a presentation tool, and countless books and seminars offer tips on how to create an effective PowerPoint presentation. Many preachers have enthusiastically adopted the PowerPoint presentation style as a way to illustrate sermons.

This practice is problematical for two reasons. First, it originated in the business world. Just like mission statements, increasing criticism is being levied in business settings at PowerPoint as a tool for presentations. All too often, people think that because they have created a glossy PowerPoint file, their presentation will be excellent. Presentations—and sermons—are outstanding when they are interesting and compelling in themselves, not simply when they are illustrated well.

And a growing number of experts believe that PowerPoint presentations seldom illustrate things well. According to Edward Tufte, an emeritus professor at Yale who specializes in the visual display of information, PowerPoint encourages "over-generalizations, imprecise statements, slogans, lightweight evidence, abrupt and thinly-argued claims."[21] Tufte cites bullet-point lists as one primary offender. He agrees that bulleted lists can help extremely disorganized speakers get organized, but he calls them "faux analytical" because they are typically too generic. Because of the brevity required on a PowerPoint slide for each item on the list, they cannot specify the critical relationships between the objects on the lists, and they cannot make clear the assumptions that lie behind the lists.[22]

Tufte argues that PowerPoint has "a distinctive, definite, well-enforced, and widely-practiced cognitive style that is contrary to serious thinking" and it "actively facilitates the making of lightweight presentations."[23] In an age when biblical literacy is at an all-time low, sermons that are lightweight presentations and lack serious thinking are not advisable. Storytelling and authentic accounts of real-life faith in action are not conducive to bulleted lists and short statements that fit on a PowerPoint slide, so the move away from sermons that resemble business presentations makes sense for our time.

If congregational leaders want to use screens in worship wisely, here is a list of things to keep in mind:

- When projecting the words to songs, enter the words into slides in exactly the order they will be sung. Don't require the technician to flip back and forth between slides as stanzas or refrains of the songs repeat.
- Think of the screen as one part of creating an environment for worship, not the only part.
- Consider the values you wish to communicate visually on the screen, perhaps serenity, beauty, peace, joy. Try to avoid a cluttered look.
- Turn the projector off for at least part of the service so that people can be encouraged to look elsewhere for a while.
- Resist the temptation to create formal PowerPoint presentations to parallel the sermon. Don't use the screen to dump information onto people.
- Remember that a good sermon comes from excellent content clearly presented, not from a good PowerPoint file.

Essential or Overvalued?

Mission statements and screens are examples of communication tools that came to congregations from the corporate world. In many places they have been enthusiastically adopted. As the business community begins to doubt the effectiveness of mission statements and PowerPoint presentations, so congregations have begun to wonder: Can a simple logo provide greater unity to congregational communications than a laboriously crafted mission statement? Can a brief slogan that can be changed with some frequency be more effective than a longer mission statement? Are worship stations and other participatory forms of worship more engaging than screens? Or are screens here to stay, but formal PowerPoint presentations aren't the best use of screens? The answers to all of these questions need to come from an assessment of the best way to communicate what the congregation values.

Questions for Reflection, Journaling, and Discussion

1. Does your congregation have a mission or vision statement, a logo, or a slogan? If so, where are they used? In what ways do they work well and provide a unifying principle for your congregation's communications? In what ways could they be used more effectively? In what ways are they bland or generic? Should their effectiveness be revisited?

2. Does your congregation use a screen in worship? In what ways does it work well? In what ways could it be improved?

3. What are the visual components of your congregation's life apart from a screen? In what ways could your congregation have a stronger visual emphasis?

9 | Congregational Communication Today

EVERYTHING ABOUT A CONGREGATION SPEAKS of its values and its identity. A congregation's heart and soul is communicated through words, photos, actions, programs, architecture, decor, the arts, and countless other aspects of congregational life. As Diana Butler Bass has noted, healthy congregations are intentional in their choices, and in our time communication choices are significant.[1]

Intentionality in communicating a congregation's heart and soul makes an impact on people both inside and outside a congregation. Members and regular attenders are stimulated to engage in relationships, serve the broader community, and draw near to God in consistent prayer and Bible study when congregations communicate clearly that they value those kinds of commitments. When a congregation is intentional about communicating who it is and what it values, people in the wider community are more likely to know whether or not they want to visit this particular congregation. Newcomers and visitors can get a clear and coherent picture of the congregation. They are more likely to see why faith commitments matter and why and how they might become involved in this congregation.

In an age of rampant consumerism, authentic and careful communication of a congregation's DNA encourages a focused commitment based in reality. I certainly wouldn't want to lure people into a congregation using glossy and deceptive strategies. At the same time I do long for congregations to do a better job

ARCHITECTURE SPEAKS

In the medieval period, many aspects of church buildings "spoke" of God's character and attributes. The tall spaces of Gothic cathedrals spoke of God's power and transcendence. The stained-glass windows reminded the viewers that God is light. The spires and pinnacles referenced the heavenly Jerusalem. Numbers of windows, doors, and columns were important, with three of anything referring to the Trinity, four referring to the four Gospels, seven to the seven days of creation, and twelve to the apostles.

Medieval cathedrals and churches were the focal point of their towns, readily visible to all. Almost everyone in a town or city would enter the building at one time or another. In some cases, the doors to huge cathedrals were quite small to convey Christ's serious words about the narrow gate. These doors were a communication strategy appropriate for that time.

Today, when congregations are no longer at the center of daily life, what do congregations want their buildings to communicate? Exterior doors, the grounds of a congregation, and the signage are increasingly important. In our time and in our communities, how do buildings communicate welcome? How do they communicate God's love and truth and other faith values?

Church buildings often convey expectations of where God will be present in a worship service. Some churches have an altar or communion table front and center, putting emphasis on the sacrament of Holy Communion. Other churches have a pulpit that towers over everything else, indicating the centrality of the preached word. What else do worship spaces "say"? How could they convey the values of faith more effectively?

using contemporary communication tools to portray who they are and what they value. I hope and pray that this book will make a contribution along those lines.

Final Questions

Because so many aspects of the new communication technologies are disconcerting, I am sure that a few questions remain after reading this book. I have collected questions that I have heard or read, and I will answer them as a way to summarize the ideas I have been writing about.

Why did you write this book?

For three years, while earning a PhD, I sat in classes focused on communication issues, read countless books and articles, and pondered the role of new communication technologies for people of faith. So often I found myself wishing I could pass on what I learned to people who are engaged in the noble task of shepherding congregations. Some people are so uneasy and unsure when dealing with the numerous new digital forms of communication, and I wished I could give them simple explanations of why they don't have to be afraid and explain for them the opportunities these new tools present. Other people fearlessly use new forms of communication, but they might not have thought a lot about how faith can be nurtured and communities developed through wise use of these tools. So I wanted to write a book for those two audiences.

In addition, it seemed obvious to me during my years as a graduate student that so many congregations convey things about themselves that simply aren't accurate because they haven't had the opportunity to think through the best ways to use these new means of communication. Their values aren't expressed clearly and their identities remain hidden because communities of faith simply don't have enough experience using these new communication tools to be able to use them wisely. I wanted to help leaders

express the heart and soul of their congregation with more preci-
sion, flair, and consistency.

*What are the biggest challenges facing congregations regarding their
communication?*

The biggest challenge facing congregations in the area of communication is the coherent expression of what they value and who
they are. That is the central focus of this book. As congregations
explore this issue, additional challenges will emerge. For some
congregations, the biggest challenge will be to overcome fears
about the new communication technologies and do the hard work
of learning how they work. Other congregations will find that their
greatest challenge lies in figuring out exactly what they do value
and who they are. Other congregations will face complex relational
issues around "ownership" of the various congregational publications and communication tools.

I want to mention an additional challenge that will probably
become more significant in most congregations. With so many
ways to send messages, the need to customize communication is
becoming more common. An Anglican minister recently told me
she has three major ways to communicate with the leaders of her
congregation. She sends e-mails to most of them, but two leaders
don't have e-mail, so she telephones them. A few leaders don't
check their e-mail very often, so she sends text messages to them.
She has noticed that one of her leaders is active on Facebook, and
this minister is wondering if she needs to get a Facebook profile
and interact with that leader through Facebook. This minister finds
it takes energy to remember the message form that works best for
each person.

*If you could give congregational leaders one piece of advice in the area
of communication, what would it be?*

Pay attention to your communication. Some leaders in congregations are so focused on what they are doing that they forget
to notice how and what they are communicating. Paying attention could mean walking through the building using the eyes of

a newcomer or reading the newsletter looking for signs of the congregation's unity and diversity. It could mean thinking about the pathway between the decisions that are made by leaders and the communication of those decisions to the congregation. Paying attention could involve reading all of the congregation's brochures or all the web pages in one sitting to get an overall sense of what is communicated. Paying attention simply means spending energy considering the way communication in the congregation happens.

Where do we start to make changes?

The first step is to observe, in a systematic way, what you are already doing in the area of communication. Collect all of the congregation's printed material. Look at the website. Observe the lobby, the worship space, the pattern of e-mails. Listen to the telephone answering machine. Look at everything through the eyes of a regular attender or member, and then look again through the eyes of a newcomer or visitor. What needs are being met? What needs are not being met?

In appendix A I have outlined a process that I call a communication audit. Involving a group of people in the audit works best, and if the audit reveals that changes need to be made, talk over those potential changes with a diverse group of congregational leaders. Decisions shouldn't be made unilaterally, as they so often are in the area of communication.

Almost all the communication decisions in our congregation have been made by one person, and she has a lot of ownership of the newsletter, the worship-announcement bulletin, and the website. How can we initiate changes without hurting her feelings?

This is a challenge that requires prayer and discernment. The first question to address prayerfully is who will conduct the communication audit and how to conduct it so that it won't appear to the communications person to be an attack on his or her work. Perhaps he or she should be included in the audit. Perhaps not. Once desired changes have been identified, the second question

A SIMPLE COMMUNICATION AUDIT

Rosemary, a Methodist minister serving a midsize congregation, gathered all the brochures and printed publications displayed in the narthex of her church to begin the process of conducting a simple communication audit. To her surprise, she noticed at first glance that none of the brochures had a single design element in common on their covers, even though they were all in-house brochures highlighting the different ministries of the congregation. They used different colored paper, different fonts, and several of them did not even have the name of the church on the cover. None of them used the church logo.

In addition, several of the brochures, as well as the monthly newsletter, did not have the church's address anywhere in the publication. Several brochures did not give an e-mail address in the contact information, even though the church secretary uses e-mail frequently for correspondence with members and visitors.

As she looked at the assemblage of printed publications, she realized that they might convey a confused message to a visitor. In addition, a newcomer might not find the contact information they needed on the brochures.

Rosemary's simple communication audit revealed significant things. For suggestions of how to conduct a similar but more comprehensive audit, see appendix A.

to address prayerfully is the best way to facilitate those changes. Sometimes initiating change incrementally is best and sometimes trying for big changes all at once is best. The essential steps are prayer, care for the people involved, and a group decision-making process that tries to stay focused on the communication issues rather than on the personalities involved.

The communications logjam in our congregation is our minister. He doesn't like computers and believes that words are the most important—if not the only—means of communicating faith values.

Again, prayer and a group process are essential. In cases where a minister is not particularly interested in computers, he or she often is perfectly content to have others in the congregation create a website and introduce visual components into congregational life. And while discussing the importance of websites and visual communication in our time, continue to affirm that the wise use of words is still vitally important.

Many ministers who were at first reluctant to endorse a congregational website have become more enthusiastic for two reasons. First, they begin to hear from new members who were drawn to the congregation because of the website. And second, they begin to experience the website as a resource they themselves can use, most frequently to access an archive of sermons. The most significant argument in favor of new forms of communication centers on the specific needs that can be met.

I know almost nothing about websites and blogs. I'm afraid that I will make terrible mistakes if I have a voice in our congregation's website or blog.

I learned about congregational websites simply by looking at them. I began by finding the websites of congregations I knew about, where my friends attended or where I had visited. After I had found all the websites of local congregations I knew about, I found the online list of the churches in my presbytery and I visited all those websites. Then I branched out and visited the websites of congregations in other cities that I read or heard about.

Most websites of congregational governing bodies, such as presbyteries, dioceses, synods, the Union for Reform Judaism, and the like, have lists of the congregations in their areas with the website addresses listed or with links to those websites. You can also use a search engine like Google and type in "churches in New York City" or "synagogues in Atlanta." You will get long lists of congregations to visit online.

Look at the home pages to get an overall impression of the page. What do you like? What do you dislike? Do the photos work well? What other graphics are used? Read the words and note the fonts and colors used. Pay attention to the links. What do those links tell you about the congregation's priorities? Visit the other pages on the website that interest you, and pay attention to what you see there. By the time you have visited a couple dozen congregational websites, I am quite sure you will have opinions about what you like and don't like, what you think works and what you think is not very effective.

Finding blogs involves a similar process. When you are looking at congregational websites, look for links to pastors' blogs. In addition, you can do a search for "blogs by pastors," "blogs by rabbis," or "blogs by ministers." The last one will get you a lot of blogs by members of parliament and other governmental ministers, but mixed in with those will be blogs by congregational ministers. You could also try adding "church" or "synagogue" to your search. Again, after you look at a couple dozen blogs by ministers or rabbis, you will have a sense of what you like and don't like.

We don't have a website. Where do we start?

Appendix B lays out a process that one church used to revamp its website, and steps on that list are relevant for congregations that are creating their first website. Begin by discussing in a group which values and which aspects of the congregation's identity are most important to communicate on the website. As a group, spend time brainstorming what you would like to see on the home page: text, photos, graphics, and links. You may want to begin collecting photos that might be used on the home page, photos that you believe convey important things about your congregation.

Spend time considering the additional pages you want to have. Based on what I have seen and heard about the way congregational websites are used, I would encourage congregations to have a page where sermons can be read or downloaded, a page of information for newcomers, and a page that helps the viewer access the congregation's values through the use of a mission statement, a brief history, or a statement of values. Separate pages for youth and children's ministries are also essential in most settings because families are always curious about what is available for their children. Another wise use of the website medium is one or more pages that describe ways to get involved in the congregation's activities, with links to contact e-mail addresses.

Will you offer online sign-ups for events? Opportunities for online contributions? Places where congregation members can post comments or questions? The more specifics you can figure out ahead of time, the more easily you will be able to make decisions about whether to hire someone to design the website or use volunteers from within the congregation. And if you have your desires for the website clearly in mind, you will be able to get a better sense of how much money you will need to spend to meet those desires.

What are the pros and cons of using volunteers versus paid people in all these communication areas?

Volunteers are obviously cheaper, and in many congregations a lot of tasks will need to be done by volunteers. Increasingly, congregations have a good number of members who are technologically savvy. One hidden cost with volunteers is that they can take a long time to get things done, and a second hidden cost is the high level of ownership that can accompany projects, which often means suggesting changes is hard. The more the congregational leaders can stay connected to the volunteers while they are working on the project, the easier it will be to make suggestions along the way.

Paid staff often, but not always, bring a higher level of competence to the task. More congregations are hiring full- or part-time web designers and audiovisual specialists. With paid staff it may be easier to make suggested changes. Again, the more engaged congregational leaders can be with paid staff during the process of creating a communication piece, the more easily suggestions can be made.

You talked about critical friends for websites. What would it look like for a congregation to have a team of critical friends?

I think critical friends are necessary for all the aspects of a congregation's communication, particularly when visual components are involved. In Western culture, visual communication is associated so strongly with advertising. So when congregations use visual communication, they often evoke the advertising medium, even if they don't particularly want to.

Critical friends for a congregation's communication might be the same group of people who conduct a communication audit and who are willing to stay on and continue to pay attention to the way things are communicated. Critical friends might be two or three individuals who are asked to make notes every time they enter your congregation's building, receive a printed publication, or look at the website.

In this book, you haven't mentioned things like press releases, radio spots, notices in local newspapers. Don't you think they have a role in congregational marketing?

This book focuses on new communication technologies and their role in congregational life. I have made the assumption that many other books address the wise use of press releases, radio spots, and newspaper notices. All of them are helpful forms of outreach that have been around a lot longer and have therefore received attention in other books about congregational marketing.

In our time, reaching into communities will take additional forms that are connected to each congregation's unique context and priorities. I read the website of one urban congregation that decided its most significant contact point with the wider community would be the arts. That congregation works hard to nurture contacts in its city's arts community and to support artists. I know of another congregation located beside an elementary school. Members of the congregation volunteer at the school helping the school nurses deal with head lice. The group that volunteers at the school call themselves "the nit busters," and they have nurtured significant connections with staff, parents, and children at the school. These individualized forms of outreach are increasingly significant in a post-Christendom culture where fewer people have a natural allegiance to churches and denominations. I greatly admire congregations who reach into their communities in unique and creative ways, and I hope many people will write books about those forms of care for the people around them. My expertise lies in new communication technologies and their implications for congregations, so this book focuses in that area.

You have said that communication constructs reality as well as reflects it. So how can the communication of our values and identity remain authentic if we are actually constructing reality as we communicate?

I believe congregational communication needs to reflect the reality of the congregation as much as possible, while realizing that what is expressed and the way it is expressed will have an influence on shaping the congregation. That means accentuating the positive is generally a good idea because it encourages the congregation to develop its strengths. But a degree of honesty about challenges and weaknesses conveys authenticity, so an overly positive approach doesn't work well in our time. A balance point between the positive and the negative aspects of each congregation's life needs to be found, probably a bit closer to the positive end.

Here is where values based on faith tradition come into play. Deep-seated values associated with the congregation's faith can be expressed, even when the congregation itself is in its infancy in acting on those values. For example, both the Christian and Jewish faiths emphasize care for the marginalized. Expressing that faith value, with a description of the efforts the congregation is making and hopes to make in that direction, can be honest, authentic, and, hopefully, inspiring as congregation members grow and develop in that direction.

Another way to describe this balance point related to authenticity is as a place between where the congregation is now and where its leaders desire to take it. It would be dishonest to talk about this congregation as a place of prayer if very little prayer goes on. But perhaps congregational leaders are trying to encourage significant participation in prayer in every setting of congregational life. This desire and commitment to growth in prayer can and should be described in congregational publications. This is both honest and helpful in encouraging the congregation to grow. And newcomers may very well want to come along and help.

What makes communication authentic?

I like the definition of authentic as "what you see is what you get." That's why it is so important for congregational communication to reflect what a congregation actually values and who it believes itself to be. Most congregational communication is not intentionally deceptive, but it is functionally deceptive because it is poorly thought-out or thrown together at the last minute.

My thesaurus lists *bogus, phony,* and *fake* as opposites to *authentic.* If a congregation wants to become more intentional in its communication, those opposites are helpful to keep in mind. Revamping the website using a series of high quality photos that are totally idealized and downright bogus as a reflection of congregational life is no more authentic than a poorly designed and boring website. Presenting a phony and overly glossy picture of congregational life is not any better than no picture at all.

What does the future of congregational communication look like?

I expect to be surprised. So many of the new communication technologies of the past few decades were virtually unimaginable before they burst on the scene. My best advice for congregational leaders is to continually ask younger members of the congregation to explain what forms of communication they are engaging in at work and at play, and where they are finding community and connections. Leaders should also ask them what they think congregations might learn and how they might wisely use new forms of communication.

I recently taught a course on communication and ministry. Most of the students were ministers and people preparing for careers in ministry, and they ranged in age from early twenties to mid-fifties. The two youngest students were kind enough to give the rest of us a tour of their Facebook and Bebo profiles and show us how those social networking websites work, and they also talked frequently about the role web-based communication plays in their lives. Their comments in class made it abundantly clear that for their generation, Internet communication is as natural as breathing and is integrally connected to the way they experience their faith communities.

Those of us in older generations need to listen hard. We need to ask questions of the younger people in our families, congregations, and workplaces. We need to listen to the answers, and then ask more questions about what we don't understand, and listen some more. And younger people of faith need to be willing to listen to their elders as well in order to enhance community. As I come to the end of this book, I wish I could write yet another one on how to listen to people in a different generation than one's own. I believe it is one of the crucial skills needed in congregations in the twenty-first century.

My hope and prayer for this book is that it has modeled assessment and analysis that can help congregations evaluate new ways to communicate. So many traditional faith values are at stake in every form of communication: Are people being treated kindly? Are marginalized people being welcomed? Is conflict being handled in an honorable fashion? Are groups of people, rather than isolated individuals, making decisions? Is the life of our faith community being nurtured? Are our values and our identity being communicated coherently and with integrity? The answers to these questions will always be significant when people of faith engage in any form of communication.

Questions for Reflection, Journaling, and Discussion

1. Which forms of communication discussed in this book make you feel uneasy or uncomfortable? What steps might you take to feel more comfortable with those communication forms?

2. In what ways does your congregation reach into its community? Which of those forms of outreach are distinctive and unique for your congregation? What forms of outreach might your congregation begin to do?

3. If you could change one thing about your congregation's communication, what would it be? What would be the steps necessary to make that change?

A | How to Conduct a Communication Audit of a Congregation

The goal in congregational communications is to convey the congregation's identity and values, its heart and soul, visually and verbally in a coherent way. The congregation's unity needs to be clear, but the diversity present in the congregation also needs to be expressed. Begin your process with prayer for God's discernment and wisdom, and continue to pray throughout the audit. A communication audit could include an examination of these components:

- Printed and electronic publications
- The building
- The telephone answering system
- Oral communication

Printed and Electronic Publications

Look at the newsletter, order of worship, announcement bulletin, pew sheets, brochures, website, blog, screen, and any other publications. Examine the verbal text and the visual components, including mission statements, slogans, logos, photos, graphics, fonts, and layout.

- Do the visual components complement the verbal text, or do they create a confusing contrast?

- Is there coherence between the various printed and electronic publications? Do they appear to describe the same congregation or are they so different that they could actually be describing different congregations?
- Examine the publications through the eyes of regular attenders as well as newcomers.
- Are the needs of both groups met?
- Are details about activities given clearly, such as location, time, and who to ask for answers to questions?
- Is the time of the worship service readily accessible?
- Is information about staff and leaders current and are e-mail addresses and phone numbers given?
- Is there information for newcomers about what to expect?
- Are both the unity and the diversity of the congregation expressed?
- What connections are made to outside organizations?

The Building

Look at signage, doors, car park, and lobby (foyer or narthex).

- In what ways are they welcoming?
- In what ways do they create unnecessary barriers?
- What impression is created?
- What forms of access are available for people with disabilities?
- In what ways are people from the community welcomed?
- Is it fairly easy to find the restrooms?

Additional issues related to the building could include considering the lighting and the quality of the sound system and the availability of hearing assistance for the hearing impaired.

The Telephone Answering System

Listen to all the messages on the congregation's voicemail system to see if the needs of potential visitors and members are met.

- Is the address of the congregation and worship service time or times given?
- Is it clear how to leave messages for various staff?

Oral Communication

Volumes have been written about sermons, and ministers often spend a lot of time considering the effectiveness of their preaching. Little attention is usually paid, however, to other forms of oral communication. In worship services, verbal announcements, minutes for mission, children's sermons, and introductions of the various components of the worship service can be evaluated for coherence as well as for expressions of the unity and diversity of the congregation. Oral communication in other settings—youth groups, adult education classes, women's and men's gatherings, annual meetings, and so forth—can also be evaluated.

- Is the oral communication clear and an appropriate length?
- Does it seem to be authentic?
- In what ways does it express the congregation's values and identity?
- Are stories and testimonies used?
- Are metaphors used wisely?

B | One Congregation's Plan for Revamping Its Website

Developed by the evangelism committee of Mount Olive Lutheran Church, Minneapolis, Minnesota, 2008.

1. Develop a comprehensive, inclusive process that will address questions derived from issues of identity and values, such as:

    *   What is the purpose of the website?
    *   What message do we want to communicate? What values and identity do we want the site to convey?
    *   To whom do we want to communicate? What are the needs and expectations of these audiences?
    *   How can the site best communicate our message to our audiences?
    *   What changes in the current site will enable us to do this job?

2. Extend an invitation to interested members to participate in a website task force that will address these questions and create a plan for the site. This task force would ensure a broad perspective on the desired design and content of the site and would help create broad ownership for the final product. Invite people from a variety of congregational committees to participate.

3. Develop specifications for design, content, and technical changes needed to carry out the task force's strategy. (Given budget restraints, the specifications might need to be "layered," so that the work could be done over the course of several years.) The plan should include specifics about how often the site will be updated with new information and sermons and who will do those updates.
4. Obtain bids from at least three vendors for the desired work.
5. With the guidance of the chosen vendor, complete the task force's strategy.
6. Make sure the site is updated regularly.

Prayer needs to be a part of every aspect of this process. At every meeting, spend time praying as a group for God's guidance in the decisions to be made. Ask for perception and insight from God's spirit as assessments are made of the congregation's values, identity, and needs.

C | For Further Reading

Bailey, Brian, with Terry Storch. *The Blogging Church: Sharing the Story of Your Church through Blogs*. San Francisco: John Wiley, 2007.

Bailey and Storch view blogs as a form of online hospitality, an inexpensive and effective tool for our time. Their helpful book gives the what, the why, and the how for congregational blogging.

Bass, Diana Butler. *The Practicing Congregation: Imagining a New Old Church*. Herndon, VA: The Alban Institute, 2004.

———. *Christianity for the Rest of Us: How the Neighborhood Church Is Transforming the Faith*. San Francisco: HarperSanFrancisco, 2006.

Bass conducted extensive research on the characteristics of healthy mainline congregations, and these two books describe the results of that research. Many of the issues she describes are closely related to the ways a congregation describes its values and identity.

Burmark, Lynell. *Visual Literacy: Learn to See, See to Learn*. Alexandria, VA: Association for Supervision and Curriculum Development, 2002.

Burmark is an educational consultant, and she argues that visual literacy needs to be a part of education in order to prepare students for the workplace, which is becoming increasingly visual. She gives helpful examples of what visual literacy looks like and how it works.

Campbell, Heidi. *Exploring Religious Community Online: We Are One in the Network*. New York: Peter Lang, 2005.
Campbell is the premier researcher on online religious community. Her research provides an understanding of how online religious community works, what people gain from it, and why it is not a threat to congregations.

Dyrness, William A. *Reformed Theology and Visual Culture: The Protestant Imagination from Calvin to Edwards*. Cambridge, UK: Cambridge University Press, 2004.
Dyrness explores the way that Reformed theology influenced the development of visual culture by impeding some forms of visual expression and encouraging others.

Gonnerman, Fred. *Getting the Word Out: The Alban Guide to Church Communications*. Herndon, VA: The Alban Institute, 2003.
Focuses on communication related to church programming and outreach, and has excellent material on how to do desktop publishing effectively, but includes little on online communication.

Hipps, Shane. *The Hidden Power of Electronic Culture: How Media Shapes Faith, the Gospel, and Church*. Grand Rapids: Zondervan, 2006.
Hipps, a Mennonite minister, had a career in advertising. Because he understands both advertising and congregational life, his insights about the significance and dangers of visual culture are helpful.

Jensen, Richard A. *Envisioning the Word: The Use of Visual Images in Preaching*. Minneapolis: Fortress Press, 2005.
Jensen describes the history and controversy of using images in preaching and offers advice about the link between exegesis and visuals.

Schultze, Quentin J. *High-Tech Worship? Using Presentational Technologies Wisely*. Grand Rapids: Baker Books, 2004.
Schultze is a Calvin College professor of communication, and he presents the opportunities and pitfalls of employing technology in congregations.

Spiegel, Aaron, Nancy Armstrong, and Brent Bill. *40 Days and 40 Bytes: Making Computers Work for Your Congregation.* Herndon, VA: The Alban Institute, 2004.

A helpful book for people who feel intimidated by computers. It contains practical information about how computers work and how they can be used in congregations.

Stephenson, Mark M. *Web-Empower Your Church: Unleashing the Power of Internet Ministry.* Nashville: Abingdon, 2006.

Contains practical ideas for the ways a website can promote and enable ministry in various areas of congregational life.

Vassallo, Wanda. *Church Communications Handbook.* Grand Rapids: Kregel, 1998.

Gives helpful information about how to develop an overall communications plan and how to discern unspoken messages that are being sent inadvertently. This book predates websites.

Wheildon, Colin. *Type and Layout: Are You Communicating or Just Making Pretty Shapes.* Mentone, Australia: The Worsley Press, 2005.

Wheildon conducted research with ordinary people to examine many factors that contribute to readability. A helpful book for people who create printed publications.

Wuthnow, Robert. *All in Sync: How Music and Art Are Revitalizing American Religion.* Berkeley: University of California Press, 2003.

Wuthnow interviewed people in an array of faith communities about their engagement with the arts.

| Notes

Introduction

1. Janet R. Cawley defines congregational identity as "what makes a congregation unique, distinct from all others" in *Who Is Our Church? Imagining Congregational Identity* (Herndon, VA: The Alban Institute, 2006), 5.

2. Diana Butler Bass, *The Practicing Congregation: Imagining a New Old Church* (Herndon, VA: The Alban Institute, 2004); Butler Bass, "Vital Signs," *Sojourners* (December 2005): 13–19; Butler Bass, *Christianity for the Rest of Us: How the Neighborhood Church Is Transforming the Faith* (San Francisco: HarperSanFrancisco, 2006).

3. These thoughts are adapted from an unpublished article by Stephen A. Hayner, Columbia Theological Seminary, entitled "The Story of the Missional Church." Numerous recent books explore the core concepts of a missional church, including *The Continuing Conversion of the Church* by Darrell L. Guder (Grand Rapids: Eerdmans, 2000) and *The Forgotten Ways: Reactivating the Missional Church* by Alan Hirsch (Grand Rapids: Brazos Press, 2006).

1 | Paradigm Shifts in Communication

1. The Gathering, Amarillo, TX, http://gatheringamarillo.org (accessed November 8, 2006; website not accessible at time of publication).

2. Jacob's Well, Kansas City, MO, www.jacobswellchurch.org (accessed October 13, 2006).

3 | Communication for Postmodern Pilgrims

1. Leonard Sweet, *Post-Modern Pilgrims: First Century Passion for the 21st Century Church* (Nashville: Broadman and Holman, 2000).

2. This view is articulated in *The Vanishing Word: The Veneration of Visual Imagery in the Postmodern World* by Arthur W. Hunt III (Wheaton, IL: Crossway Books, 2004).

3. Lynell Burmark, *Visual Literacy: Learn to See, See to Learn* (Alexandria, VA: Association for Supervision and Curriculum Development, 2002), 5.

4. Sweet, *Post-Modern Pilgrims*, 92.

5. Shane Hipps, "But Now I See," *Leadership Journal* (Summer 2007): 23. Excerpted from *The Hidden Power of Electronic Culture: How Media Shapes Faith, the Gospel, and Church* (Grand Rapids: Zondervan, 2006).

6. Ibid., 24.

7. Robert Wuthnow, *All in Sync: How Music and Art Are Revitalizing American Religion* (Berkeley: University of California Press, 2003), 16.

8. Ibid., xiv–xv.

9. MissionGathering, San Diego, CA, http://www.missiongathering .com/home.php (accessed October 14, 2006).

4 | Websites

1. Heidi Campbell, "Approaches to Religious Research in Computer-Mediated Communication," ed. Jolyon P. Mitchell and Sophia Marriage, *Mediating Religion: Conversations in Media, Religion, and Culture* (New York: T & T Clark, 2003), 216.

5 | Communicating Right Now

1. This insight comes from a colleague of mine, Erica Baffelli, who teaches Japanese religions. She notes that the 2007 Technorati report on blogs (http://www.sifry.com/alerts/archives/000493.html) reveals that

more blogs are written in Japanese than in English. This is remarkable because many more people speak English than Japanese as their first language, and English is used professionally by many people who speak it as a second or third language. My colleague also reports that Japanese "diary literature" (*nikki bungaku* in Japanese) emerged during the Heian period (794–1192 CE). See Earl Miner, "The Traditions and Forms of the Japanese Poetic Diary," *Pacific Coast Philology* 3 (1968): 38–48.

2. Brian Bailey and Terry Storch, *The Blogging Church* (San Francisco: John Wiley and Sons, 2007), 38.

3. Ibid., 57. This list is adapted from Bailey and Storch's list of suggestions.

6 | Online Community

1. Heidi Campbell, "A New Forum for Religion: Spiritual Pilgrimage Online," *TransMissions*, Summer 2001, pp. 8-9; Campbell, "Congregation of the Disembodied," ed. Mark J. P. Wolf, *Virtual Morality* (London: Peter Lang, 2003); Campbell, *Exploring Religious Community Online: We Are One in the Network* (New York: Peter Lang, 2005).

7 | The Gifts and Perils of Desktop Publishing

1. Sam McManis, "What Does Your Choice of Typeface Say about You?" *Otago Daily Times* (January 9, 2008): 23. Originally published in the *Sacramento Bee*.

2. Ibid.

3. Many studies of readability of various fonts in various sizes have been conducted. If you do an Internet search for "font readability," you can access a variety of opinions and research results. Results of these studies vary widely. Some studies indicate that sans serif fonts are more readable for blocks of text, others indicate that serif fonts are more readable, and still others show that sans serif and serif fonts are about the same in readability. The studies do seem to indicate that within the range of 8 to 12 points font size, larger font sizes are more readable. (Note that

this does not continue upward. Size 18 fonts would not be more readable than 12 point fonts for blocks of text.)

4. A point is the smallest unit of measure in typography, with 72 points to the inch. One point equals .3527 mm.

5. Space does not permit me to write at length about wise use of color. It is a complicated topic, and I strongly recommend that if a congregation wants to use a color printer routinely for newsletters and brochures, then the person designing the publications needs to do some training or at least some reading. Lynell Burmark addresses the use of color in *Visual Literacy*. Another good resource is *Type and Layout: Are You Communicating or Just Making Pretty Shapes* by Colin Wheildon (Mentone, Australia: The Worsley Press, 2005).

6. PDF stands for portable document format, a format created by Adobe Systems. Adobe Reader can be downloaded from the Internet for free. Adobe Acrobat, the complete software package intended for graphic designers, can also be used to read and create PDF files. Macs offer the option of saving documents as PDF files. For PCs, readily available software can be used to save documents in PDF. Usually, saving a document in PDF is preferable to scanning the document because the resulting image will likely be sharper and clearer.

8 | Two Controversial Tools

1. Gil Rendle and Alice Mann, *Holy Conversations: Strategic Planning as a Spiritual Practice for Congregations* (Herndon, VA: The Alban Institute, 2003), 84.

2. Ibid.

3. Ibid., 85.

4. In "Mission Statements, Bizspeak and Bromides" by Kelley Holland, *New York Times*, September 23, 2007, http://www.nytimes.com.

5. University Presbyterian Church, Seattle, WA, http://www.upc.org/ (accessed March 15, 2008).

6. First Congregational United Church of Christ, Washington, DC, http://www.fccuccdc.org/ (accessed March 15, 2008).

7. United Church of Hayward, CA, http://www.haywarducc.org/ (accessed March 15, 2008).

8. Pasadena Presbyterian Church, CA, http://www.ppc.net/ (accessed March 15, 2008).

9. Sunshine Community Church, Grand Rapids, MI, http://www.sunshinechurch.org (accessed March 15, 2008).

10. Fair Haven Ministries, Hudsonville, MI, http://www.fhmin.org/index.html (accessed March 15, 2008).

11. St. Paul's Collegiate Church at Storrs, Storrs Mansfield, CT, http://www.spcc-storrs.org/ (accessed March 15, 2008).

12. Lyndale United Church of Christ, Minneapolis, MN, http://www.lyndaleucc.org/ (accessed March 15, 2008).

13. The Bridge, Pontiac, MI, http://www.thebridgechurch.com/ (accessed March 15, 2008).

14. New Life Church, Springfield, MO, http://www.new-lifechurch.org/index.html (accessed March 15, 2008).

15. Lord of Light Lutheran Church, Ann Arbor, MI, http://www.lordoflight.org/ (accessed March 15, 2008).

16. College Church of the Nazarene, Olathe, KS, http://www.collegechurch.com/ (accessed March 15, 2008).

17. The People's Church, Franklin, TN, http://www.thepeopleschurch.org (accessed March 15, 2008).

18. Vineyard Church North Phoenix, Glendale, AZ, http://vineyardnorthphoenix.com/ (accessed March 15, 2008).

19. Bob Sitze, an author who explores the connections between biology and theology, explains the issues connected with multitasking: "Your brain can pay attention to only one thing at a time. The much-vaunted multitasking attributed to human brains is another falsely applied technological metaphor. Although computers may be able to do several things at the same time, multitasking in humans may be more accurately described as your brain's increasingly rapid shiftings of information between foreground and background. Younger and more technologically dependent individuals may appear to be multitasking when, in fact, their brains are just working quickly. At least for a few years." See *Your Brain Goes to Church: Neuroscience and Congregational Life* (Herndon, VA: The Alban Institute, 2005), 81.

20. All of the statistics cited from the *Leadership Journal* survey come from Eric Reed, "Preaching by Faith and by Sight," *Leadership Journal* (Summer 2007): 25–27.

21. Edward R. Tufte, *The Cognitive Style of PowerPoint* (Cheshire, CT: Graphics Press, 2003), 4.

22. Ibid., 5, 6.

23. Ibid., 26.

9 | Congregational Communication Today

1. Bass, *Christianity for the Rest of Us*.